Praise for
Chuck Runyon, and Dave Mortensen

Daniel H. Pink
New York Times and *Wall Street Journal* Best-Selling Author of *Drive*

"Chuck Runyon and Dave Mortensen love their work at Anytime Fitness—and they're passionate about guiding others into a love of their own work. Drawing on their vast experience, they teach the power of 'the four Ps'—people, purpose, profits, and play—so that you can find the joy in your career. This book will answer all your questions about how to grow a corporate culture that your employees will love."

John R. DiJulius III
Author of *The Customer Service Revolution*

"The culture that Chuck and Dave have built is astonishing. They've created a community of franchisees, leaders, team members, and customers with a fanaticism I've rarely come across. If you're a leader who wants to grow your business by growing your people, then you need to absorb every word of *Love Work*."

David Horsager
Best-Selling Author of *The Trust Edge*

"*Love Work* is a riveting account of how people, purpose, profits, and play can rev up the engine of any successful organization. And what really makes it all work is the fact that Chuck and Dave have achieved a hard-earned trust with their people, as well as in their own unique partnership."

Michael Solberg
President & CEO, Bell Bank

"I've known Chuck and Dave for years, and *Love Work* perfectly bottles the incredible culture they've built at Anytime Fitness. If anyone has the magic formula for high performance, it's them. And it's all laid out in these pages."

Robert Cresanti
President, International Franchise Association

"Anytime Fitness is one of the fastest-growing franchisors in their industry, and *Love Work* shows why. Quite simply, Chuck and Dave know what makes people tick and how to inspire any organization to perform at the highest level."

LOVE WORK

CHUCK RUNYON
DAVE MORTENSEN
with Marc Conklin

LOVE WORK

Inspire a high-performing work culture at the center of people, purpose, profits, and play®

BEACHED WHALE PRESS

LOVE WORK

This publication is designed to provide general information regarding the subject matter covered. However, laws and practices often vary from state to state and are subject to change. Be sure to review and understand the laws and regulations in each state in which you conduct business.

The authors and publisher have taken reasonable precautions in the preparation of this book and believe the facts presented within are accurate as of the date it was written. However, neither the authors nor the publisher assumes any responsibility for any errors or omissions. The authors and publisher specifically disclaim any liability resulting from the use or application of the information contained in this book, and the information is not intended to serve as legal, financial, or other professional advice related to individual situations.

Copyright ©2017 Chuck Runyon and Dave Mortenson.
All rights reserved.

People, Purpose, Profits, Play® is a registered trademark of Anytime Fitness, LLC and is used with permission herein.

No part of this book may be reproduced, stored in a retrieval system, or transmitted by any means, electronic, mechanical, photocopying, recording, or otherwise, without written permission from the copyright holder.

If you purchase this book without a cover, you should be aware that this book may have been stolen property and reported as "unsold and destroyed" by the publisher. In such case, neither the author nor the publisher has received any payment for this "stripped book."

Published by Beached Whale Press.

For ordering information or special discounts for bulk purchases, please visit:
www.PeoplePurposeProfitsPlay.com

Cover design, composition & editing by Accelerate Media Partners, LLC

Hard Back ISBN: 978-0-9991743-0-2

Library of Congress Control Number: 2017948743

BUS025000 BUSINESS & ECONOMICS / Entrepreneurship

Printed in the United States of America.

Heart♥First
EXERCISING GENEROSITY

The authors are contributing proceeds from the sale of this book to Operation HeartFirst, the charitable giving program of Anytime Fitness: Dedicated to helping U.S. military veterans own and operate Anytime Fitness franchises.

Dedication

To the millions of Anytime Fitness employees, franchisees, and members we've known through the years and throughout the world. Your passion and collaboration have steered this brand to the center of people, purpose, profits, and play®. And together, we've created the most remarkable life-changing stories the fitness industry has ever seen.

Table of Contents

Acknowledgments......................................xi

Foreword...xiii

Introduction.......................................xvii

    Chapter 1: What's Changed?..........................1

I. People..9

    Chapter 2: How Much Do You *Really* Value People?..........15

    Chapter 3: The 5 Levels of a People-Oriented Work Culture....27

    Chapter 4: Designing a People Culture.....................37

    Chapter 5: An Outside Perspective: John Donahoe...........59

    Moving to Action: People................................63

    A Story to Tell: Rachele Jordan..........................68

    A Story to Tell: "The Planking Grandma"..................70

II. Purpose..73

    Chapter 6: Purpose Starts with You........................77

    Chapter 7: Building a Tattoo-Worthy Brand.................85

Chapter 8: An Outside Perspective: Michael Solberg 103

Moving to Action: Purpose 107
A Story to Tell: Jeff O'Mara 111
A Story to Tell: Mary Thoma & The Golden Girls 114

III. Profits 117

Chapter 9: The Only P That Matters? 123
Chapter 10: The Currency of Lifestyle 143
Chapter 11: Profits 101 151
Chapter 12: An Outside Perspective: Suzanne DiBianca 163

Moving to Action: Profits 167
A Story to Tell: Eric Keller 171

IV. Play 173

Chapter 13: The Benefits of Play 181
Chapter 14: Playing It Right 193
Chapter 15: An Outside Perspective: Dr. Peter Diamandis 203

Moving to Action: Play 207
A Story to Tell: Tressa Dokken 212
A Story to Tell: Marc Conklin 214

Chapter 16: Applying the 4 Ps 217

Assessing Your P-ocity 226
One More Story to Tell: Brian & Lisa Bazely 231
Final Words of Advice 234

About the Authors 237

Acknowledgments

This book wouldn't have been possible without the support of too many people to mention, but we'll try.

To our entire Self Esteem Brands team, for your talent, dedication, and purposeful work. You literally change lives, and it's been deeply gratifying to work beside you every day.

To Anytime Fitness and Waxing the City franchise owners: You continue to inspire and push us, and we look forward to seeing both brands continue to evolve with your feedback and collaboration. We're grateful for your commitment, and you have our admiration and respect.

To our vendors: Many of you have gone above and beyond providing a product or service, and we thank you for helping this brand get the world to a healthier place.

To our board of directors: Brian Smith, Brent Knudson, Erik Morris, Steve Romaniello, Debra Jensen, Martin Brok, and the Roark Capital team. We appreciate your investments of both time and money, as well as your thoughtful approach to enrich all stakeholders.

To Chuck Modell, for being a sage cornerman during the many rounds of negotiations and challenges outlined in this book.

To our book-writing team: Marc Conklin, for helping us organize so many different thoughts and experiences into one (hopefully readable) book, and for your playful and creative influence over the years. To Carol Grannis, for your commitment to developing people and your ability to translate ideas into actions. To our "Outside Perspective" contributors, who believed in our message enough to help us validate it. To Reed Bilbray, for your expertise and insights on the book business. To our inner circle of readers, for your valuable time and invaluable feedback. And to the Anytime Fitness employees, franchisees, and members who contributed their own amazing stories—without which we couldn't possibly tell ours. While we shared only a fraction of the stories we received (we could have filled four books), reading yours gave us goosebumps and internal tattoos.

Finally, to our incredible spouses, Shannon and Nicolle, and children (nine total): Thank you for supporting us, putting up with us, and joining us on this crazy ride. The families of entrepreneurs make so many sacrifices without getting any credit. This book is about designing a culture to Love Work, but even better, we live in another book called *Love Home*. Each of you adds new pages to that book every day, and we look forward to writing even more in the years to come.

Foreword

by Ken Schmidt, Former Director of Communications for Harley-Davidson Motor Company

When I was Harley-Davidson's mouthpiece, I was asked about tattoos all the time, because everyone knows that "Harley" and "tattoo" have been wedded for over a century. Harley tats are a world-famous expression of *profound* loyalty—emphasis on profound, because trust me, you'll never see a Harley-tattooed rider on a non-Harley bike. Ever.

It's very rare to feel so strongly about something that you'll get a tattoo to express it, and it's even more rare for that something to be a business. Harley prides itself on this kind of fanaticism, and the assumption is that there's nothing else quite like it. So imagine my surprise when I found myself at an Anytime Fitness annual conference watching five tattoo artists inking purple logos onto people—not just members, but franchise owners, employees, and vendors—while dozens more waited in long lines.

I had been invited to the conference to speak about my philosophy on competitiveness and my belief that when a business creates an energized customer and employee base, it can dominate competitors that compete simply by opening their doors and doing whatever's expected. Any concerns I had about my message resonating with the audience flew out the window the moment I saw those long tattoo lines and felt the excitement in the air. I'd never seen this outside the Harley world. And while I was surprised, I also knew that I was probably the only human on the planet who needed no explanation for what was happening.

When I shared my delight at this with Chuck Runyon and Dave Mortensen, they were quick to deflect any personal credit. They said what I had just witnessed was proof of their organization's commitment to a mix of 4 Ps: people, purpose, profits, and play. "What about the fifth P, passion?" I asked. "What do you think drives those 4 Ps?" Chuck said, and that was just the kind of answer I was hoping for. Because what's happening under the skin of the tattooed loyalist is an intense passion that no one—not even Shakespeare or The Beatles—has ever been able to define. Words can't always explain what we feel in our hearts, but we know passion when we see and feel it. A tattoo allows us to express that love in a way that people instantly understand.

The truth is, every association we have with a business—good or bad—is a reflection of that business's culture. And every business culture reflects its leadership. We're naturally skeptical about how businesses and people describe themselves, but we always believe and act on what we hear from others who we know and trust. In other words: Don't tell me you're passionate, because everyone says that. *Show* me you're passionate, and then when I tell others about you, they'll believe me.

An authentically passionate culture is the strongest competitive advantage a business can have, because all humans seek joy. We're attracted to passionate people, and our passion grows when we share it with others. It's not just contagious, it's infectious. And magnetically attractive. When people share their passion with others about a business, that business grows at the expense of its competitors.

During my time at the Anytime Fitness conference, I came to understand all I needed to know about the company, its leadership, and its people. Passionate leaders inspire passionate work cultures that breed passionate customers and employees who love coming to work in the morning. It's a beautiful thing that both Harley and Anytime Fitness get, and *Love Work* gives me hope that more people will have the tools to join the movement.

If anyone knows how to harness the power of passion to create a high-performing work culture, vocal customers, and energized employees, it's Chuck and Dave. They can talk the talk because they've walked the walk. And we're fortunate that instead of keeping their secrets close to the vest, they've chosen to bottle them here in an accessible and entertaining way.

By the time you've turned the last page of *Love Work*, you'll be energized to build a more positive and energized culture in your business, starting right now. Heck, it might even inspire you to get a tattoo.

Introduction

Imagine this: You've barely entered your 40s, and someone offers you a check so big that you could retire today. It's the American Dream, right? Quit your job, cash out, and spend the rest of your life on a golf course. Well, that's exactly where we found ourselves in April 2009. The American Dream was offered to us on a silver platter. And we turned it down.

Seven years earlier, we had teamed up with a longtime friend and business partner to start a new gym franchise called Anytime Fitness. Now we had 1,000 clubs open—a growth milestone only 1 percent of franchises ever reach—and private equity firms were jockeying for a stake in our company. For a couple of high school–educated kids from the blue-collar east side of St. Paul, Minnesota, it was like winning the lottery.

Yet something didn't feel right. Instead of imagining ourselves taking the money and escaping to a tropical island somewhere, we found ourselves on an emotional rollercoaster that ultimately led us to confront a big question:

What's the purpose of work?

This is something most people never really think about, and up to that point, neither had we. Our parents had made their livings driving trucks, working for the railroad, and slinging burgers at McDonald's. Like most folks, we viewed work through a purely practical lens: You trade time and effort for slips of paper that pay your bills. The truth is, most people simply tolerate work as something that funds the other parts of their lives. And if you see work as a means to an end, then you probably think we were idiots for not grabbing that investor money.

But we were after something different, something more. We both sensed that there was an untraveled, unmarked path ahead that was both terrifying and exciting. Where did it lead? What would we experience? Could work actually be a life-enriching experience filled with personal development, adventure, and fun that delivered benefits beyond a paycheck? We didn't have the answers, but we needed to find out.

Truth be told, we also knew that Anytime Fitness wasn't in the best shape at that point—at least not for the long term. Knowing that other gyms would try to copy our always-open business model, we had operated with a "grow or die" mentality and opened an average of one gym every 2.5 days. That kind of expansion comes at a cost, and the cracks were beginning to show.

The biggest fissures were among the business partners themselves. The two of us were usually on the same page. But as a trio, we had become like those bands featured on VH1's "Behind the Music." On the surface, we were making beautiful music, smashing old business categories, and rocking the fitness world.

But backstage, things were falling apart.

Over time, these differences had become increasingly hard to ignore. Our partner wanted to pocket most of the profits we were generating; we wanted to invest it in people, infrastructure, technology, and tools. He wanted a personal return on investment; we were after something more ambitious: We wanted to harness fitness to change people's lives—not just physically, but mentally and emotionally as well. We didn't want people *only* to lose weight; we wanted them to boost their overall self-esteem and achieve greater personal fulfillment. We wanted to help people achieve what we called "ROEI: Return on Emotional Investment."

And we had a long way to go. Dysfunction among the three owners had begun to infect our entire company culture. We felt out of alignment with our core values, and our work culture wasn't where we wanted it to be. In addition to this (or maybe because of it), we were coming off our worst six months of business. Growth was slowing. Franchisee unrest was on the rise. The entire country was mired in recession, and the business we had built from scratch was in danger of imploding. Given the primal choice between fight or flight, flight was actually looking pretty damn good at that point.

But something made us want to fight instead. And in the fall of 2009, we made a critical decision: Instead of cashing in, we would buy out our third partner by signing our names to a substantial loan. This wasn't as easy as it sounds. The entire world was teetering on the edge of economic collapse, and banks were extremely tight with money. The buyout we eventually settled on carried Tony Soprano–like interest rates. So basically, instead of waking up in a hammock in the Caribbean, we agreed to stay in Minnesota and wake up every morning to another $13,000 interest payment. Every day. For two years.

    Was this buyout a risky thing to do? Yes—borderline insane, looking back on it. We would need to work our asses off while our partner would never have to work again. But we were energized by the fact that we hadn't said no to something; we had said yes. Yes to an even more purposeful vision. Yes to changing the entire culture of work. Yes to taking our business to the next level of growth, revenue, and impact. Yes to making money by making a difference in people's lives. We didn't have a textbook or a map to work from, but we did have our instincts. And those instincts now pointed in one direction: *Be different. Go against the grain. You have more to learn and more to offer. Embrace uncertainty. Inspire people to love their work.*

    That attitude manifested itself in multiple ways. When it came to the business model, we decided that while other gyms relied on signing up thousands of members and then hoping that they wouldn't show up to work out, we would focus on boosting engagement and helping people get real results. When it came to members, we decided that while other gyms turned away people whose health situations presented challenges to their personal trainers, we would embrace empathy and open our doors to everyone. When it came to our corporate staff, we decided to focus on trust—refusing to create thick employee handbooks or crank out onerous policies that punish the 99 percent to prevent the actions of the 1. We wanted to keep a keen eye on the bottom line, but we also wanted to reinvest in operations, infrastructure, and employee development. Most of all, we decided that our culture needed to regain and expand on the spirit of playfulness it had started with, because life is too damn short not to have fun.

What followed was a stretch of remarkable growth, unique shared experiences, and impressive accolades that changed a lot of lives, especially ours.

As of this writing, Anytime Fitness now has nearly 4,000 gyms in 29 countries serving over 3 million members. We've been ranked as the #1 global franchise and the best place to work in Minnesota. We've created a parent company, Self Esteem Brands, with a bold mission to improve the self-esteem of the world. And in 2012, we partnered with the founders of Waxing the City (a body-waxing franchise) to provide new opportunities for their franchisees, studio personnel, and clients. We've helped millions of people around the globe not only lose weight and run marathons but also gain new confidence, improve their emotional well-being, throw away their expensive prescription drugs, and even manage and overcome post-traumatic stress disorder (PTSD). Over 3,000 of our franchisees, employees, and members feel so strongly about our brand that they've actually tattooed our logo onto their bodies—a passion most brands can only dream of.

Despite the fact that fitness and franchising are two of the world's most competitive business spaces, we're now one of only 16 franchise brands to achieve our size and geographical reach (to put that in perspective, only 12 people have ever walked on the moon). Plus, no one has done it faster than we have. In fact, we'll soon become one of just a handful of brands in history—in any industry—to reach 5,000 open franchises on six (possibly seven) continents. And when Jeff Bezos or Elon Musk finally colonizes Mars, you can bet we'll be there to get people to a healthier place.

But perhaps no single day better encapsulated our journey than Dec. 19, 2013. On that day, exactly four years after we bought out our former partner, all of the following happened:

- *Entrepreneur* magazine named Anytime Fitness the world's #1 franchise for the first time, beating out fitness competitors like Snap and Gold's Gym, but also titans like McDonald's, Hampton by Hilton, and 7-Eleven.

- We bought a 38-acre parcel of land to build the amazing new corporate campus that we now call home.

- We sold new Anytime Fitness territories in Hong Kong, Singapore, Malaysia, the Philippines, and China.

- We signed a Letter of Intent to sell 40 percent of the company to a strategic partner who shared our core values, at a financial valuation over four times that of our deal in 2009.

That last item might sound like one of those deals we turned down in 2009. But the circumstances couldn't have been more different. Four years earlier, we had been pretty naive about private equity; now we knew how to free up cash without sacrificing control. True, our appetite for risk had tempered a little (we had nine kids between us to send to college), but we had also grown to value outside strategic counsel. Bottom line:

It was time to trade less operational freedom for more financial freedom and expertise.

In choosing our strategic partner, we also took a highly unusual step: Like Jerry Maguire writing his mission statement about better ways to represent professional athletes, we composed an eight-page "Investor Manifesto" outlining our beliefs on business, leadership, and life. We made competing firms read and understand this document, but we even took it one important step further by insisting that they write one of their own. We didn't do this just to make financial firms jump through hoops (although that was fun). We did it because we were after something more than capital. Money can seem like a commodity, but we knew it had the potential to help every gym owner, member, employee, and community where we operated. If we were going to continue to make a difference in the world, we needed a partner who shared our values.

The Manifesto helped us begin to answer the question that nagged us back in the spring of 2009: "What's the purpose of work?" In a way, it was also the first draft of this book. In writing it, we had to reflect on where we'd come from, where we were, and where we wanted to go—not just as entrepreneurs, but as people. We had built a culture at the intersection of four elements: people, purpose, profits, and play®. And while each of those elements is important and powerful on its own, the chemical reaction of combining them is absolutely life-changing.

The 4 Ps still guide our business and our lives, and now we want to share their secrets with you. You're not alone in the struggles of starting or running a business, and we want this book to feel like a team of experts coaching you to create a positive, high-performing culture in your organization.

You don't have to be a prominent business leader or wealthy entrepreneur to find happiness and meaning. You just need to align your true values with your employees, your company, and any other organization you care deeply about.

    The journey begins by learning the true virtues of people, purpose, profits, and play, and by living your life smack-dab in the middle of them. So let's get started, and let's start loving work!

—Chuck & Dave

— CHAPTER 1 —

What's Changed?

> *"Culture eats strategy for breakfast."*
> —Peter Drucker

As we started putting this book together, a fundamental question kept nagging us:

Why are we even talking about workplace culture?

•

Our parents and grandparents grew up in a world that barely gave a second thought to this issue, so what's changed? First, a definition: Culture is the personality of your business. It both reflects and influences how your people behave, and it creates a feedback loop that can be either positive or negative. Although no two organizations have the same culture, its basic elements don't change: mission, vision, values, leadership style, workplace practices (hiring, training, benefits), work environment, and communication.

Business leaders will identify, study, and copy any behavior that gives them an edge. And in the last four decades, workplace culture has consistently risen to the top as a powerful competitive advantage across all industries. Here's why.

1. **The data.** The more people study high-performing companies, the more "culture" comes up as a key factor.[1] This likely started with the Total Quality Management (TQM) craze in the 1980s. TQM taught people that listening to employees and valuing their ideas is an important practice for a successful organization. And these values show up in positive cultures.

2. **EQ vs. IQ.** Traditionally, we've valued IQ in business leaders. But the more we know about effective leadership, the more we see the importance of emotional intelligence, or EQ. Leaders with high EQs demonstrate self-awareness, self-management, social awareness, and social management. They listen. They collaborate. And they care about others' needs and perspectives. These behaviors also form the foundation of high-performing workplace cultures.

3. **The "Best of" List Explosion.** The companies our parents and grandparents worked for weren't aggressively studied and measured against their peers. Today, we're bombarded with "Best Places to Work" and other lists. And especially in the age of social media, making the cut is critical for finding good people, staying competitive, and winning in the marketplace.

4 **Generational shifts.** It's impossible to know exactly why one generation comes to value something more than another, but it happens. The fact is, while all generations prefer workplace cultures that are fair, ethical, straightforward, and collaborative, Gen Xers and Millennials also want theirs to be "friendly and social"—something not on the radars of Baby Boomers and Traditionals.[2] You can spend your time wondering why this is the case, but it's far more useful to simply accept it and ask, "How are we supporting these values within our own culture?"

We've seen all these trends come to fruition in our own business. When we started in 2002, we created the convenient gym category. On paper, the barriers to entry were low. All you had to do was rent 5,000 square feet in a local strip mall, load it with fitness equipment, provide 24-hour access, and sell memberships. That simplicity allowed us to scale fast, but it also made it extraordinarily easy for competitors to emerge. Sure enough, within three years of our launch, more than a dozen copycats had flooded the market. You'd think we were dead in the water. But fast-forward to today, and only a few of those imitators still exist. Anytime Fitness is nearly three times bigger than its closest competitor, and about 35 times bigger than the one after that.

So why is there such a large gap today between us and our competitors? Why do we have the largest global presence? What's the X factor that has spurred our continued growth while others have hit a ceiling? You could say it's the fact that we were first to market in the US, but we haven't been first in some other countries, and we've still won there. You could say it was our private equity infusion, which provided capital, resources, and expertise to grow. But one of our competitors made a large private equity deal before we did, so that's clearly not the secret either.

We think the big difference is our culture, and that's not an easy thing to copy.

GROWTH COMPARISON

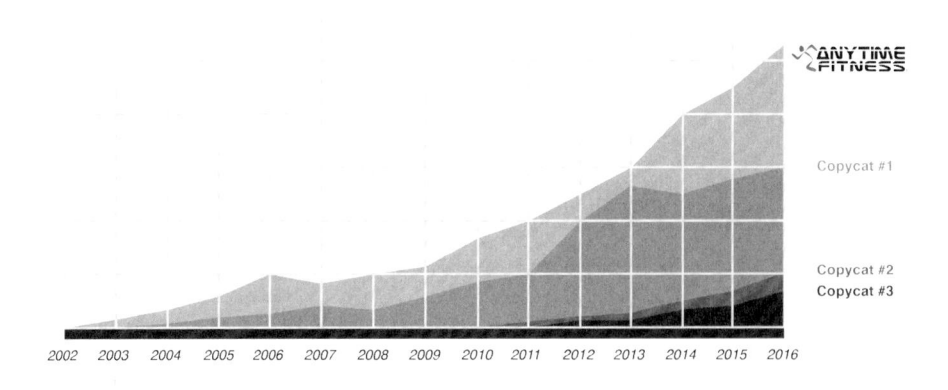

- ANYTIME FITNESS
- Copycat #1
- Copycat #2
- Copycat #3

2002 2003 2004 2005 2006 2007 2008 2009 2010 2011 2012 2013 2014 2015 2016

- ANYTIME FITNESS
- Copycat #3
- Copycat #2
- Copycat #1

You might have heard the phrase at the top of this chapter, usually attributed to management guru Peter Drucker: "Culture eats strategy for breakfast." While we agree with that statement, it's probably more helpful to see culture and strategy as linked and inseparable. As a leader, the workplace culture you help create plays a huge role in determining whether or not you win in the marketplace, and winning in the marketplace feeds a winning culture. In other words, culture is strategy, and strategy is culture. It's not a competition; it's a collaboration.

The Scourge of "Undertime"

The other major change fueling the focus on culture is the growing study of workplace engagement. Polling company Gallup tracks this metric for the US, and to give you an idea how important they think it is, their website publishes employee engagement measurements along with presidential approval ratings, real unemployment rates, and the latest numbers on consumer spending and economic confidence—*every day*.

What does Gallup's research tell us about how much we love work? We wish the news was better. The truth is, nearly 70 percent of Americans aren't engaged with their jobs, and this hasn't changed significantly in years.[3] Think about that for a second. Most people spend at least half their lives at work, and they see a majority of that time as a passionless exchange of money for time. How depressing is that?

In our view, life includes many occupations, but only one

job: to live a remarkable existence filled with fun, happiness, healthy relationships, personal fulfillment, and making a positive impact on others. How can you do that if most of your life fails to inspire you, and even fills you with feelings of boredom, dread, and anxiety?

This is bad news for everybody who draws a paycheck, but it should also ring major alarm bells for business leaders. Most companies devote massive resources to fighting public policy battles around issues like taxes, regulations, and rules around overtime pay. But in doing so, they tend to ignore the actual biggest killer of productivity and profitability—the one that lurks in every corner of their organization: **undertime.**

Undertime is our word for a business leader's public enemy #1: the amount of money you pay for disengaged workers who are only present physically. A product of workplace disengagement, undertime includes symptoms such as disconnection, disillusion, displeasure, dissatisfaction, and distraction. And it's highly contagious, so you need to address it before it infects your entire workforce.

It's easy to think of undertime as a problem at *other* organizations, but employee engagement studies show that it's likely an issue at yours as well. According to Salary.com:[4]

- 89% of employees say they waste time at work.
- 31% waste roughly 1 hour a day.
- 16% waste roughly 2 hours a day.
- 4% waste at least half the average workday on non-work-related tasks.

No matter what industry you're in, undertime is your Kryptonite—leading to lost hours, lost revenue, and lost opportunities. The good news is, culture is your Superman. And what's the key to creating and sustaining a high-performance culture? Boosting employee engagement through the 4 Ps. So let's dive into them one at a time.

---

[1] W. Edwards Deming, *Out of the Crisis*, 1982; Peter R. Scholtes, *The Team Handbook: How to Use Teams to Improve Quality*, 1988; Edgar H. Schein, *Organizational Culture and Leadership*, 1991.

[2] Anick Tolbize, "Generational Differences in the Workplace," 2008. http://rtc.umn.edu/docs/2_18_Gen_diff_workplace.pdf.

[3] Gallup Daily, "Real Unemployment." Accessed May 29, 2017. www.gallup.com.

[4] Aaron Gouveia, "2014 Wasting Time at Work Survey," www.salary.com/2014-wasting-time-at-work/slide/2/.

— PART I —

People

"You don't build a business.
You build people, and then the people
build the business."

—Zig Ziglar

Formative People Moment

•

When I was in high school and living with my brother in Minot, North Dakota, I had a wrestling coach who seemed to know that maybe I wasn't getting enough to eat at home. Sometimes after weigh-ins, he'd take me aside and say, "Hey, David, how about you and I get a burger?"

As a coach, he cared about more than winning. He cared about his wrestlers on and off the mat. And while this was a simple gesture, it was also a life-changing one that I've never forgotten.

—Dave

When we launched Anytime Fitness, the first iPod had just been launched, and Facebook and the iPhone were still five years in the future. It felt like a completely different time, and we were launching a completely different fitness club model. After spending years in the trenches visiting hundreds of fitness clubs, we had come up with a new breed of gym franchise: convenient locations, 24/7 access, just the equipment you like to use, all for an affordable monthly fee.

But as we talked about in the previous chapter, business models can only get you so far—especially when others can steal your ideas. In the end, we haven't succeeded because we have better treadmills. We've succeeded because we've built a better culture. And while the uniqueness of that culture can be tied to hundreds of small details and decisions—from website and club designs, to marketing, training, even how a customer service agent answers the phone—none of that works without great execution. And great execution requires the talent, communication, and collaboration of great people.

When we asked "What's the purpose of work?" back in 2009, we had already started down a more people-oriented path. And it made sense. The simple fact is, we spend a third of our lives at work—more than we do with our spouses and children. Given that time commitment, shouldn't we feel some personal fulfillment in our jobs? Shouldn't work be a place where we feel truly awake and fully engaged?

As leaders, we can make that happen, and it all starts with changing the way we think about our organizations. It's one thing to use the word "people" in our mission and vision statements.

But until we see "human beings" instead of "employees," see "innovators" instead of "headcount," and see "investments" instead of "cost centers," the truth is, we're not really there.

To succeed as individuals, organizations, communities, and a planet, we need to value people like never before. And to be clear, your motivation in doing so doesn't have to come from some lofty moral perch. For us, the original catalyst in focusing on people wasn't some grand, world-changing vision. Frankly, we just knew we were a couple of idiots who needed help.

・・・

Speaking of people (and needing help), you'll notice that in keeping with our philosophy of collaboration, we're going to end this and the other P sections with three special features that bring in outside voices to complement our message:

1. In **"An Outside Perspective,"** a prominent business leader from an industry other than fitness will offer his or her unique thoughts and actions related to that particular P.

2. In **"Moving to Action,"** leadership expert Carol Grannis will help you translate our ideas into immediate actions within your organization. Carol's insights on team development and communication strategies have consistently helped us get the most out of our people and our culture.

3. In **"A Story to Tell,"** Anytime Fitness employees, members, and franchise owners will relate their amazing personal stories related to the 4 Ps.

In this P (People) section:

- We'll challenge your assumptions on what it means to value people.

- We'll define five levels of people-oriented work cultures.

- We'll go over some practical ways to operationalize a more people-oriented focus.

- We'll share a valuable outside perspective from an internationally respected business leader famous for building people-friendly cultures where you'd least expect them.

And it all starts with one question . . .

— CHAPTER 2 —

How Much Do You *Really* Value People?

"You'll never have to miss life's most important moments."

—Chuck & Dave's Promise to Anytime Fitness Employees

After a 69-year-old grandma nearly dies from a variety of health issues, a personal trainer helps her regain her health— and set the Guinness World Record for planking.[5]

•

A personal trainer is approached by a woman who says, "I need you to help me right now or I'm going to kill myself." Today, she's 100 lbs. lighter and credits the trainer with saving her life.

•

When he learns that one of his members has dentures that no longer fit after she lost 180 lbs., a gym owner organizes a member fundraiser so that she can finally smile about her amazing accomplishment.

•

After a man loses his legs and fingertips to a flesh-eating bacteria, he's turned down by six gyms. When one finally welcomes him, the personal trainers train him for an endurance race and eventually carry him across the finish line.

•

When a gym owner finds out that one of her members needs a new kidney, she goes under the knife and donates one of her own.

•

These stories may sound like a series of over-the-top Hollywood movie pitches, but they're all true tales involving real Anytime Fitness gym owners, trainers, and members. There's a lot more where those came from, and they always warm our hearts. But they also point to something important that it took us far too long to learn: We're all in the people business. For the first three years of Anytime Fitness, we thought we were in the fitness business. In the next three, we came to realize that we were in the franchise business. But for the last nine, we've definitely come to realize that it's all about people.

You might write this sentiment off as a bunch of touch-feely B.S. And we get that. Everybody talks about the importance of people, *yada yada*. But the truth is, whatever your age, gender, race, or ethnicity, we all strive for significance. We all need to matter. We all want to love and laugh and live a life filled with deep and memorable experiences. If you employ a human being, and if you are a human being, then you're in the people business, period.

And let's be clear: Valuing people isn't just a nice thing to do; it works. In cutthroat Silicon Valley, does success always go to the tech companies with the fastest and best technology platforms? No, it actually goes to those who recruit and retain the best people—and get the most out of them. Companies like Google shower their people with perks like free meals, transportation, unlimited vacation, and time to work on personal projects. We've visited Google's campus, and the expense involved is staggering. But it's also clearly worth it. Google understands and embraces the gravitational force of culture, and that's why they keep winning.

Trainer Dave Candra coaches Betty Lou Sweeney on her world-class planking form.

Mike Rike helps Lydia Dziubanek overcome life-threatening depression.

LOVE WORK

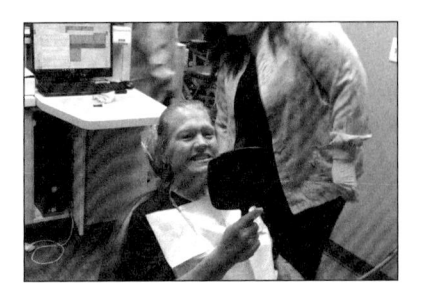

Mary Hertzel finally gets a new set of dentures thanks to help from her fellow gym members.

Roy Davis is helped across a mud run finish line by his Anytime Fitness friends.

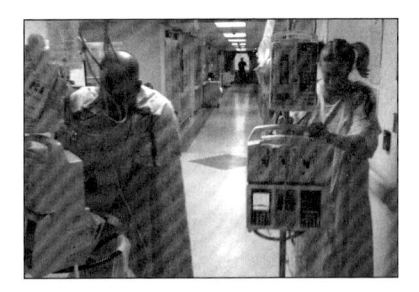

Anytime Fitness club owner Radley West donates a kidney to one of her members.

"Employers" vs. "Leaders"

Before Anytime Fitness, we were basically business-turnaround artists. Along with our third partner, we ran a membership promotion company that contracted with distressed fitness centers in the US, Canada, and Australia. We would arrive at a struggling health club, implement a marketing and sales campaign to generate hundreds of memberships quickly, then move on to the next one. It was an exciting job that took us to a new city every two months (perfect when you're in your mid-20s), and we built that company into a profitable business that lasted over a decade.

In the end, though, we have to admit that while our business was successful, it wasn't *special*. We could have been bigger and more profitable, and we could have made a bigger impact on people's lives. But instead, we made the same mistake that virtually every other company makes: In our business and in our clients' businesses, we saw people as headcount, so naturally we saw our own employees as little more than a cost center. The result was high turnover, inconsistent morale, uneven performance, and difficulty differentiating ourselves from every other employer in town. Like a lot of other businesses, we cared mostly about winning new customers today. We didn't yet understand that we were actually in a talent war to build the best team for tomorrow.

We'll tackle how to become a people-centric organization in the next chapter, "The 5 Levels of a People-Oriented Work Culture." But first, we want you to understand four key distinctions between employers and leaders.

#1. Employers see employees. Leaders see human beings.

One day, two sisters who work for our company learned that their father had been diagnosed with late-stage cancer. He was given just a few months to live, and the sisters—who happened to work in the same department—immediately exhausted their vacation and personal time off (PTO) to spend as much time with him as possible. The father ended up outliving his prognosis, and when he reached his final days, the sisters were out of options to get off work.

This presented a serious problem for their manager. Rigidly sticking to the rules seemed heartless. But if she bent the rules and gave the sisters more PTO, then she would be accused of playing favorites, setting a bad precedent, and unfairly burdening the rest of the department. Despite what her gut was saying, she decided to stick to company policy, because isn't that what a strong leader does?

We weren't aware of any of this until one of the sisters' co-workers approached us and offered to give up some of her own PTO to help her colleagues out—a touching gesture that definitely earned our attention. After getting the manager's perspective, we decided that the right thing to do was to give the sisters as much time off as they needed. As a result, the sisters were able to hold their dad's hand during his last week of life. The whole department banded together in support and didn't skip a beat.

As a leader, you have to realize that when people leave work, a new story begins for them. Single parents might be juggling homework projects with their kids. A son or daughter might be assisting their aging parents. Others could be planning a wedding, preparing for an impending birth, practicing for a weekend gig with their band, or volunteering as a youth soccer coach. If you see yourself strictly as an employer, then you don't know (or don't care) about these activities. But if you see yourself as a leader, then you know and appreciate the whole person—not just the employee—and see these life events as opportunities to support their entire life.

Don't get us wrong. There's certainly a need for rules—especially as your company grows. But policies and employee manuals are the Tin Men of corporate culture: They lack heart. When your team feels stuck between a manual and a heart place, go with the heart. This mindset has molded our approach to investing in the personal and professional growth of our team members. And in our experience, if employees are happier in their personal lives, they'll show up to work with an energy that's positively contagious.

#2. Employers see expenses. Leaders see assets.

As fitness marketing consultants, we saw employees as a cost center. Even with Anytime Fitness, a key element of our early business model was the ability to eliminate expenses around managing people. Our unique access and surveillance systems allowed members to use our gyms safely without staff present, which allowed owners to minimize payroll costs by employing just one person for 20–50 hours a week. This seemed to make sense, because what business owner actually enjoys the time and expense of constantly managing employee turnover?

Over time, we learned that seeing people as an expense isn't simply inaccurate; it also kills profitability and growth. Say your small company does $500,000 in annual revenue and you spend $175,000 on payroll. If you see that money purely as an expense, then you're constantly thinking, "If I could just reduce payroll by X percent, I could boost profitability by XX percent." So you spend your time looking for ways to lower compensation, reduce headcount, or cut people's hours. In a sense, you start seeing people as the enemy.

We grew quickly in the early years of Anytime Fitness, but we also hit the same growth wall as many of our competitors. The key decision that ultimately allowed us to smash through it was a shift in our mindset. When you start to see people as allies, partners, and assets, then your brain rewires itself. Instead of trying to minimize an expense, you start looking for ways to invest in an asset—just as you would your machinery, technology, infrastructure, or property.

The idea of investing in people was one of the primary friction points leading up to our partner buyout in 2009. If we had adopted a culture that saw employees as replaceable pawns that stifled profits, then we would have suffered the same fate as our competitors. Luckily, we were willing to learn from our mistakes and start investing in a team of smart, creative, and caring people.

Some company leaders refuse to make this shift, because they see it as too risky. "Technology stays put, but employees are free to leave, so why help them better their own career and take that knowledge to a competitor?" they argue. It's true that people are less predictable than technology (most of the time), but there's also no better way to push a good person out the door than by not supporting them. We've invested in plenty of employees who have eventually left the company. And guess what? Many of them have come back.

#3. Employers see shortcomings. Leaders see significance.

Two years after Chuck graduated from high school, he went back to coach the freshmen basketball team. His school was known for hockey (one of its alums was Herb Brooks, coach of the 1980 "Miracle" US Olympic team), so to say that the basketball program was an ugly stepchild would be an insult to ugly stepchildren.

Only 10 kids tried out for the team, so everyone made it. As you might expect, some of the boys had solid basketball IQs, while others were "Rudys": not as naturally talented but extremely hard-working. Chuck enjoyed working with each player to bring out his best, but over time, he noticed a negative team chemistry taking shape. The more talented players had formed their own clique and weren't supporting the other guys.

This was a problem on many levels, but the most immediate concern was the fact that the team's next opponent was Central High School. In the world of St. Paul basketball back then,

Central was the Soviet hockey team of the 1980s. They had a star player on their freshman team who was better than most varsity players in the Twin Cities. He was tall and athletic, with off-the-charts abilities in ball handling, rebounding, and scoring.

Knowing that a standard man-to-man defense wouldn't work on this guy, Chuck told his team that they were going to employ the "diamond and one" strategy, in which four players form a diamond zone, while the fifth hounds the opponent's best player all over the court. The goal is simple: Keep the star player from getting the ball, tire him out, and frustrate the hell out of him.

To do this, the team needed a constant stream of fresh legs, and that presented the perfect opportunity for each player to contribute. Chuck told his Rudys that they were the key to winning this game. All they had to do was give everything they had for 90 seconds at a time and keep Central High School's Michael Jordan from getting the ball. Chuck even made it into a contest, saying he would track how many times their star touched the ball and which defender was the best at denying him. Something about this strategy touched a positive nerve, because the Rudys were amped up in the locker room—and once the game started, they found an extra gear.

In the movie version of this story, David beats Goliath. In reality, Chuck's team lost the game 55–50 (it was close to the end). More important than the score, though, was the effect that his "strategy of significance" had on team culture and morale. Every player understood that they didn't have to be the star, because every rebound, block, charge, and steal had an impact. Team chemistry remained strong for the rest of that season, and the players continued to engage with and support one another. The Rudys earned a new level of respect from the other players. And in the practices and games that followed, clique-y behavior was replaced by cheers and high-fives all around.

This coaching experience taught Chuck more about leadership and employee engagement in a shorter time than anything since. Mostly, it drove home the fact that everyone wants to get a meaningful stat in the scorebook—or, as Steve Jobs famously put it, "put a dent in the universe." Getting people to feel their personal significance is a leader's greatest responsibility, and people perform better when they understand how they can contribute. Whether you're a coach, manager, or CEO, one of your most important jobs is to help people understand how their performance makes an impact. Insignificance breeds apathy and erodes effort. Significance creates a positive cycle. It creates empowerment. Empowerment leads to better performance. And performance fuels an even greater sense of significance.

#4. Employers act like cops. Leaders act like coaches.

Speaking of coaching, that brings us to our last point. When you think about it, most of the time, a police officer's job is to respond to (and correct) negative events. The same can be said for soldiers, ER doctors, and many of society's other first responders. We value the police officer who stops the criminal, the firefighter who puts out the fire, the soldier who defeats the threat, and the doctor who cures disease.

The problem is that when your job is to fix something that's broken, it's hard not to see the wrong in every situation. As the saying goes: If all you have is a hammer, then everything starts to look like a nail. As a business owner, that's an unhealthy mindset to have. If you think like a cop and see yourself as a problem solver, then you end up spending most of your time looking for problems instead of creating a culture that prevents problems from happening in the first place. We've all had that boss who only talked to us when we did something wrong. Did that make you feel empowered and energized, or defeated and drained?

Coaches and leaders have a totally different mindset from this—at least the good ones do. Their job is to get a team to perform, so they work hard on developing their people. Do they point out mistakes? Of course. And they don't hand out positive reinforcement like candy. When you have a coach's mindset, you're honest, you offer balanced feedback, and you help your players accentuate their strengths while improving their weaknesses. That's what good leadership is all about. And that's what empowers you to create a people-oriented work culture.

---

[5] See the full story of "The Planking Grandma" at the end of this section (if you want to feel both inspired and inadequate).

— CHAPTER 3 —

The 5 Levels of a People-Oriented Work Culture

> "If you plan on being anything less than you are capable of being, you will probably be unhappy all the days of your life."
>
> —Abraham Maslow

Imagine a CEO who takes over a struggling company to return it to profitability. Coming from a dog-eat-dog background, she decides that employees have become too complacent and entitled, so she introduces hyper-accountability into the culture. On day one, she mandates that the heads of each business unit start to rank each of their employees as "top," "good," "average," "below average," or "poor" performers—with the understanding that all poor performers will be fired and replaced.

The CEO expects that the new system will wake people up, push them to work harder, and improve the company's financial performance. Instead, people become aware of the system and shift into self-preservation mode. They fight for their personal survival. They protect their turf. And to bolster their rankings, they actually avoid working with brighter and more experienced colleagues.

As a result, company culture takes a turn toward fear and backstabbing. Collaboration ends. Deadlines are missed. Fingers are pointed. Productivity tanks. Turnover accelerates. Innovation stagnates. Competitors lick their chops. And eventually, the only person fired is the CEO.

•

Stories like this one have played out at dozens of businesses over the years. The Machiavellian process we described is known as "stack ranking," and extreme versions of it have been introduced at Microsoft and other Fortune 500 companies, only to be discontinued when it started hurting productivity. Stack ranking is the perfect example of an "anti-people" policy. Rather than lifting employees up and encouraging the knowledge sharing that leads to innovation, it appeals to the worst of human nature and leaves destruction in its wake.

Most small to midsize businesses don't adopt this kind of management style, but how "enlightened" is your business when it comes to its overall relationship to people? Now that we've covered things from a leadership perspective, let's take a look at your organization as a whole.

All companies fall into one of five people-centric categories—very similar to the famous pyramid known as Abraham Maslow's "Hierarchy of Needs." Maslow looked at human needs on five levels and believed that a person could climb to the next level only after they had achieved the one beneath it. At the bottom, he listed the fundamental requirements for food, water, warmth, and rest. Then came safety and security. Then love, intimacy, and friendship. Then self-worth and accomplishment. And finally, the Holy Grail of "self-actualization": achieving your true potential.

We think a similar hierarchy exists for companies, based on how enlightened they are in terms of people. To reach your full potential as an organization, you need to determine which level you sit at today, then work toward a corporate self-actualization that benefits your people, your organization, and society at large.

Level 1: The "Pay and Benefits" Company

The most common type of relationship between organizations and their people is based on the simple trade of money for effort. As an employer, you hire employees to do anything that a machine or piece of software can't do better. You basically rent the employee's brain or body to execute a fair but passionless exchange of value, and call it a day.

Most of our ancestors worked these jobs, some of them their entire lives. Chances are, you've experienced one or two of them yourself, probably during your teenage years—like when Dave was a sandwich-making machine at a fast-food chain and Chuck was a VHS-tape collector at a movie-rental store. You wouldn't expect these types of jobs to offer much in the way of personal fulfillment, and we certainly didn't feel any. Maybe that's why we were both fired for mouthing off (or maybe our rebellious attitudes were a sign that we needed to be our own bosses). The point is: This Level 1 arrangement is a good foundation, but on its own, it does little to produce high engagement and performance.

Our Anytime Fitness Level 1 Promise

We give our people the financial means to provide for themselves and their families.

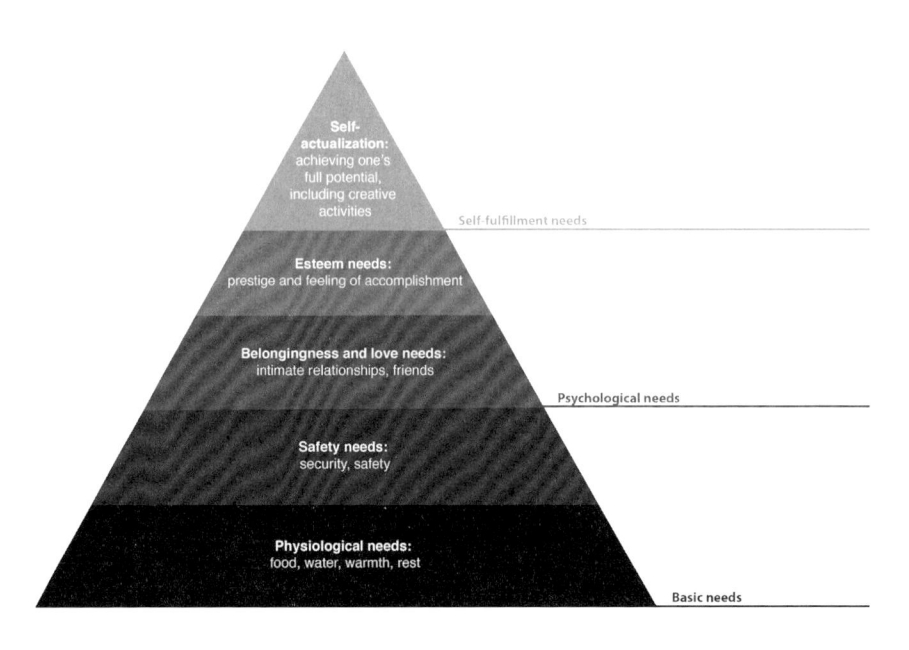

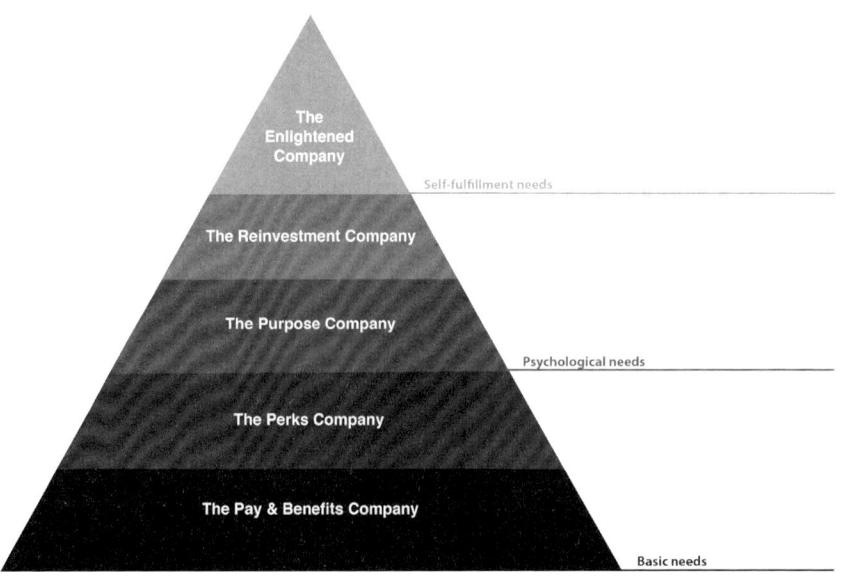

Maslow's Hierarchy of Needs

- **Self-actualization:** achieving one's full potential, including creative activities — *Self-fulfillment needs*
- **Esteem needs:** prestige and feeling of accomplishment
- **Belongingness and love needs:** intimate relationships, friends — *Psychological needs*
- **Safety needs:** security, safety
- **Physiological needs:** food, water, warmth, rest — *Basic needs*

Company Hierarchy

- The Enlightened Company — *Self-fulfillment needs*
- The Reinvestment Company
- The Purpose Company — *Psychological needs*
- The Perks Company
- The Pay & Benefits Company — *Basic needs*

Level 2: The "Perks" Company

If you're this type of organization, you're living in the Land of Better Than Average. Maybe during a tight labor market, you developed a mission around "attracting and retaining the best and brightest people." As a result, you've set employee compensation slightly higher than the industry average. If the competition for people is especially tough, you've also added benefits beyond health insurance, vacation, and a generous 401(k) contribution match.

Maybe you have a campus that offers a dry cleaner, day care service, and coffee shop. Or maybe you provide greater flexibility than your competitors when it comes to working remotely. Not surprisingly, our headquarters building features a fully operational Anytime Fitness gym. We also provide time each day for employees to take part in physical activities like yoga and boot camps. And we sponsor team events where bonds can form that really pay off when a project goes sideways. Some Level 2 employers also give employees company time to work on inspirational personal projects, but only in the hope that the resulting idea will ultimately benefit the company.

This is great for employees and employers, but it still rises only to the second level of the pyramid. There are still three levels to climb.

Our Anytime Fitness Level 2 Promise

We strive every day to understand, appreciate, and support the highest values and priorities of our people.

Level 3: The "Purpose" Company

You'll see much more on purpose in the next section, but because purpose and people are so intertwined, we'll offer a sneak preview here. Especially as Millennials have entered the workforce, more and more companies have come to embrace what we call "the economics of passion." The basic idea is that if employees feel a sense of on-the-job mission that rises above simply earning a paycheck, then they'll be more engaged, work harder, and show more creativity.

Research backs this up.[6] A survey from Deloitte found that 73 percent of employees who work at companies they see as "purpose driven" feel engaged in their work, whereas only 23 percent of employees feel engaged if they don't see that bigger purpose. The survey defined a purpose-driven company as one that has "an important objective that creates meaningful impact for stakeholders," including not only the company's customers and investors but also its employees and the larger community.

If you're a purpose-driven organization, then you've probably spent time trying to define and communicate the "why" behind your company. And you might also see the value in sharing inspirational stories about how your company and employees are changing the world. As we've seen firsthand, people respond to these efforts. They feel a greater sense of satisfaction on a day-to-day basis, which in turn lowers turnover and improves your ability to attract better talent. But even if your culture is fueled by an authentic sense of purpose, you're still only at Level 3.

Our Anytime Fitness Level 3 Promise

We make sure that our people understand the ways in which they change others' lives, and we share examples of their impact as often as possible.

Level 4: The "Reinvestment" Company

A few years ago, one of our employees suffered from two fears that most people can identify with: heights and public speaking. She thought these phobias were unrelated and incurable. Let's just say that with a little "push," she got a new perspective on the world: She jumped out of an airplane at 13,000 feet during a company-sponsored skydiving experience. Not only did she survive this experience (along with about a dozen others), but she literally lived to tell about it. Getting over her "heights hump" boosted her overall confidence, and today she's a strong public speaker who also tackles speaking for company activities.

If Level 3 is talking the talk, then Level 4 is walking the walk. This is where companies actively reinvest in their people. Notice we didn't say "employees"; we said "people." Because at this level, you truly see people first and employees second. This isn't the same as setting aside a budget for training. It's about reinvesting your resources into helping your people improve themselves mentally, physically, emotionally, and even (broadly defined) spiritually.

At Level 3, you offer resources directly related to an individual's job, but you also provide classes on seemingly non-job-related topics and invite experts to talk about various skills or hobbies. We once brought in a personal money expert to help our people make better financial choices and lower stress at both home and work. We hired a behavior-change expert to give a seminar on being a better spouse, parent, and human being. We once even brought in a coupon expert, because hey, what better way to help people save thousands of dollars a year than teaching them about coupons?

    The point is simple: When people are better outside of work, they're better inside of work.

Our Anytime Fitness Level 4 Promise

We invest in our people as people, not just as employees and franchisees.

Level 5: The "Enlightened" Company

    Every path to enlightenment ultimately leads to a nirvana-like ideal that's as difficult to define as it is to achieve. We know that a Level 1 company says, "I pay you; you do what I pay you for." A Level 2 company says, "I pay you more than the other guys and give you some added perks; you work a little harder and stay a little longer." A Level 3 company says, "I pay you, shower you with perks, and give you a sense of purpose; you work harder and more creatively to make this company better." And a Level 4 company says, "I expect you to improve this company, but I also want to make you better as well." But with Level 5, you only know it when you're there.

Once you reach the highest level of valuing people, you achieve an intense and magical chemistry that blurs the lines between home and work. In a Level 5 company, teamwork fosters trust, communication, problem-solving, and innovation. Internal silos are flattened. Employees with equal rank work together without needing a higher-ranking executive to mediate between them or resolve conflict. Employees don't just give their time and expertise; they give their hearts and souls. Most significantly, you actually hear the word "love" applied to work—as in "I love my co-workers," "I love this company and what we do," and "I love work."

In this type of relationship, you're not just renting a brain or body, and you're going well beyond purpose and reinvestment. Your people might think about work during their personal time— not because of extreme pressure or unreasonable demands, but because they have a genuine feeling of satisfaction in performing purposeful work. To use a music analogy, you're finally in a place where it's about the music, not the musician.

Our Anytime Fitness Level 5 Promise

We try like hell to achieve this, even though we know we might not get there every day.

It's the Journey, Not the Destination

The journey to Level 5 might sound difficult, not to mention expensive. At Anytime Fitness, we feel like we achieve Level 5 most days, but there's always room to get better. Regardless, we can honestly say that the benefits we've seen along the way have far outweighed the costs.

Once you start to move up the pyramid, you begin to see a culture of learning and teamwork emerge. This culture minimizes intra-company friction points that cost far more in productivity than your investments in creating it. For instance, when we have to pick one department's priority over another, we find that the "losing" department rallies around the project instead of sandbagging their colleagues to win the budget next time. That outcome may not show up on the balance sheet, but how much is it worth to your business?

Being truly people-oriented requires a commitment to leadership and resources that won't always seem directly related to return on investment. It's certainly fair for a CEO to ask, "How will offering a gardening class make my company better at selling widgets?" But remember, you're in the people business. And if you see your employees first as mothers, fathers, brothers, sisters, sons, daughters, citizens—and even part-time gardeners—then investing in the whole person makes sense, both on and off the balance sheet.

Great, you say, but what can you do on a tactical level to build a people-oriented culture? Glad you asked . . .

---

[6] Adam Vaccaro, "How a Sense of Purpose Boosts Engagement," Inc., http://www.inc.com/adam-vaccaro/purpose-employee-engagement.html.

— CHAPTER 4 —

Designing a People Culture

> "Hiring people is an art,
> not a science, and you can't tell from
> a résumé if someone will fit into the
> corporate culture."
>
> —Howard Schultz

The "5 Levels" give you a 30,000-foot view into how you see people today. But how do you move up the pyramid? How do you change what you do in your day-to-day life as a business leader to reach the next level?

After we decided to build a higher-performing culture at Anytime Fitness, we faced the reality that not everyone in our organization shared our values. At the same time, we knew that while some people might be able to change their attitude over time, others might not, and we needed to make sure that every new team member we brought in was a good fit.

When it comes to people, your culture is your most powerful magnet. And you don't want that magnet to attract anything and anyone; only the most valuable assets. In our experience, that means designing a people-oriented culture across five key areas:

1. *Hiring*
2. *Onboarding*
3. *The Day-to-Day*
4. *Evaluation and Feedback*
5. *Investment*

Hiring: "The Culture Fit"

Super Bowls end in February, but they actually start a year earlier, when NFL teams hold their scouting combine and run players though one of the world's most rigorous evaluation processes. During these events, athletes are poked, prodded, measured, and thrown into a battery of mental and physical tests—all so that a team can decide whether to draft them in April and invest millions of dollars into salaries, team doctors, trainers, position coaches, office personnel, and film specialists.

Despite this scrutiny, not every high draft pick makes an impact, and sometimes a low pick overachieves. Tom Brady—probably the greatest quarterback of all time—famously wasn't drafted until the sixth round. And the fact that he has thrived with New England might not be an accident. Nearly everyone who enters the Patriots' system seems to do well. Why is that?

In football, as in business, identifying strong talent is only half of the equation. The other half is knowing whether a person is a good cultural fit with your organization. At Anytime Fitness, we evaluate people using a high-performance grid. The vertical axis measures what we affectionately call "ability to get shit done," and this line basically lines up with a person's skills relative to the job. The horizontal axis is our culture line, and it describes the more subjective fit between that person and the organization—including shared behaviors and values.

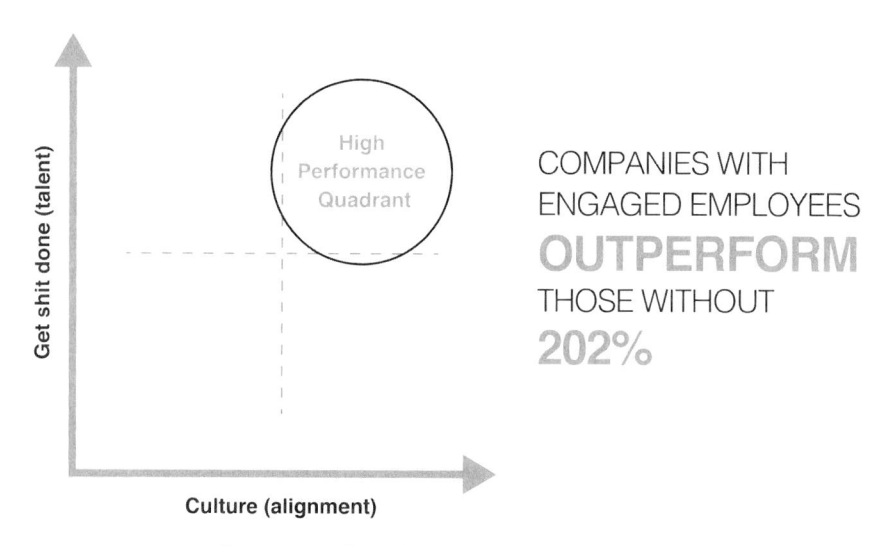

Get shit done (talent) ↑ — High Performance Quadrant — Culture (alignment) →

COMPANIES WITH ENGAGED EMPLOYEES OUTPERFORM THOSE WITHOUT 202%

Most organizations already know the skills their company needs, but "hiring for culture" is something leaders often grossly underestimate. Every job applicant who walks through your door brings a unique mix of nature and nurture—genetics coupled with decades of life experiences that have shaped their values, behaviors, and attitudes. We all have a self-interest that pushes us to find opportunities that fit our ambitions. Similarly, your company is wired with an organizational self-interest to create and grow profits within an environment that reflects many things, including the founder's or CEO's values, leadership personalities, and market-driven circumstances.

The best approach to recruiting isn't to hire the highest-skilled workers and then hope that they'll adopt your company's values. It's bringing in people who already embrace a similar set of values, behaviors, and working styles. When an individual's self-interest and personality overlap with your organization's self-interest and culture, then you arrive at what we call "Collective Interest." And that's the sweet spot of high engagement you need.

ENGAGEMENT

SELF-INTEREST   **COLLECTIVE INTEREST**   **COMPANY INTEREST**

WHERE THE MAGIC HAPPENS

In the early days of Anytime Fitness, we could hire for culture fairly easily, because we were small enough to handle new hires personally. Now that we've grown, however, we've gotten more systematic about it. So today, we have The Law of the Fives: a five-step hiring process in which we measure candidates against five distinct cultural values.

The 5-Step Hiring Process

Every candidate goes through the following process—or at least starts it.

1. We conduct an initial "gatekeeper" interview to see if the candidate should make it to round 2.

2. We convene a small-group interview with the actual team members the candidate would be collaborating with.

3. We give the candidate a project to complete and send to the group. For example: "Write a letter on why you want to work here" or "Make a five-minute video or 10-slide PowerPoint presentation that tells us who you are." (This can provide a window into the candidate's personality, as well as show their creative and technical skills.)

4. We execute background, referral, and/or social media checks.

5. We have the candidate interview with team members from other departments, including a senior leader.

5 Traits to Look For in a Potential Employee

During this process, we look for the following key traits:

1. ***Self-Awareness***
   People with strong self-awareness usually possess higher emotional intelligence, which means they have better interactions with their peers. Self-aware people know their

strengths and weaknesses, and they can anticipate how they'll behave in certain situations. This equates to a better ability to stay motivated, manage stress, and maintain balance.

Questions to help determine a candidate's level of self-awareness:

- What are your top three strengths and weaknesses? (Be honest.)

- What are some past mistakes or regrets, and what did you learn from them?

- If we were introduced to a past co-worker or boss of yours who didn't enjoy working with you, what would they say about you?

2. **Sense of Humor**

We place a high value on team members who can take their work seriously without taking themselves seriously. Why? Because life is too damn short not to have laughter in the workplace. Humor helps foster a sense of play, brings people together, fuels collaboration, alleviates stress, and brings joy to everyone's day. In an interview, we may ask a candidate to complete a project that gives us a glimpse into their silly side. We might also ask them to share a time when people have laughed both with them and at them, because in many ways, the ability to laugh at yourself is the ultimate sign of personal security and stability.

3. Competitiveness

Business is brutally competitive, and we want to win. So we want people who value winning, are seriously bothered by losing, and have shown strong self-motivation in the past. During the interview process, we look for a history of team sports or individual ambitions that have included elements of competition, teamwork, self-improvement, and "coachability" (openness to the feedback of colleagues and mentors).

4. Passion

Passion is hard to measure and easy to fake in an interview, but eventually you learn to recognize when someone has an authentic fire in their belly by the hot, flickering light in their eyes. During the interview process, we'll ask people to tell us what they're passionate about and why. We look for answers that include hobbies, charitable causes, or other ideas they believe in. Then we ask them about working for our company, and we look for their eyes to start flickering.

5. Selflessness

Anytime Fitness offers people the chance to "get to a healthier place" (#G2HP, more than just our tagline) through a better job, better franchise opportunities, and better health. To do this at a high level requires natural empathy, a willingness to sacrifice, and an ability to put the needs of others ahead of their own. During the interview process, we ask candidates to tell us about their experiences with volunteering, helping charitable organizations, coaching, caregiving, or other ways that they've put their own needs aside to impact others.

You may have heard the adage "slow to hire, quick to fire," and we completely agree with this (though we learned the hard way for too many years). This axiom is even more evident in a small business: When an employee is let go, the team often isn't big enough to absorb the duties, so the owner has to do the work until a new hire is found. Because of this, the owner is sometimes reluctant to replace someone. As a result, he or she sometimes retains a low performer for too long and watches the business underperform over time.

Savvy leaders recognize when they've made the wrong hire, and they swiftly look to upgrade their team. Over time, higher performance will offer a payback on the energy and costs required to hire and onboard the new employees.

Onboarding: Making It Consistent

Any talk about onboarding at Anytime Fitness has to start with a story from one of our Halloween parties. Halloween is a big deal at our corporate headquarters. Not only do our employees dress up, but we also host a party that includes skits from new employees (more on this in Chapter 13, "The Benefits of Play"). One day during our early years, Chuck noticed that a UPS delivery man was watching the Halloween festivities, packages in hand, with a big smile on his face. Chuck approached the guy and bragged, "I bet UPS doesn't have Halloween parties like this. By the way, who's the package for?" Chuck heard others start to laugh, until it suddenly dawned on him that the guy was actually an Anytime employee dressed as a UPS guy. In fact, he had been with us for over a month.

This raised all kinds of troubling questions for us: How many other employees had been hired that we hadn't even met yet? How do new employees learn about our company values, how we got here, and where we're going? When do they learn about payroll, benefits, 401(k)s, and vacation? Do they all get a computer, a cell phone, and full access to the building, and do they have access to sensitive data? Have they even been inside one of our clubs? When your business grows fast, it's easy to lose track of these things.

The next day, we asked our various departments how they introduce new employees to the business, and every answer we received was different. The result was a standardized onboarding process that we've kept consistent ever since. Looking back, we wish we had done this sooner, because it's such an invaluable tool in helping new team members adjust to their environment and build their confidence early.

Your process should be customized to the size and nature of your business, but make sure you have one. To get you started, here's our recommended **Onboarding Checklist:**

Day 1

- Make sure your team is prepared to welcome the new team member.

- Make sure workspace is ready with the resources needed for their job (computers, uniforms, etc.).

- Plan to take the new team member out to lunch with any team members who are available.

- Walk the new team member through the history of the company. How did it come to be? Discuss the products, services, values, mission statements, and purpose of the organization. Talk about the industry and competition.

- Introduce the new team member to other areas of the company.

- Assign a workplace "go-to person" for the first month.

- Have the new team member fill out all paperwork, and explain benefits, payroll, and other employee policies.

First Week/Month

- Review specific business/division/team goals with the new team member.

- Review the main goals of this position and define what success looks like 30/90/120 days out.

- Identify one to three development goals for the new team member during their first year.

- Have the new team member's manager schedule weekly or biweekly one-on-one sessions. This is an ideal time to create a foundation of communication and trust.

- Intensify the training for the new team member's responsibilities.

- Provide a deeper understanding of the stakeholders they serve.

- Share company stories that establish the organization's expectations, behavior, and values.

- Have the new team member read articles or watch videos that broaden company or industry knowledge.

- Within the new person's larger team, complete a trust-building task such as the popular "River of Life" exercise.

The Day-to-Day: Communication, Alignment, Trust

Soon after our partner buyout in 2009, we decided that we needed an outside perspective to move our culture in a more positive direction. Knowing that employees aren't always completely honest when speaking directly to leadership, we brought in a professional psychologist to serve as a comprehensive organizational therapist. For weeks, she sat down in private with each employee, gathering feedback to uncover the good, the bad, and the ugly. This humbling experience taught us that the ultimate success of any relationship (business or personal) depends on talking openly and frequently, reaching agreement on key issues, and feeling confident that you can always rely on the other person. We've come to call this "CAT": **Communication, Alignment, Trust.**

In the early years of a start-up, CAT is relatively easy to achieve. Amid the constant chaos of a small group fighting for success, a certain intimacy develops. Everybody adopts an egalitarian, "all hands on deck" work ethic fueled by high energy, engagement, and caffeine. During this phase, it's fairly easy to communicate opportunities, address problems, and keep everyone aligned on important objectives. The underdog spirit of a tight team naturally builds trust.

But as a company grows, people need more formal processes around strategic planning, responsibilities, reporting, and internal communication. As new team members come in, most founders and business owners struggle to scale their businesses the right way. They get pulled farther and farther away from the front lines. New processes make the business suddenly feel rigid, slow, and bureaucratic. And many early team members get frustrated, because the days of quick decisions, ad hoc solutions, and tight-knit chemistry are gone.

This is where the cracks in an organization's culture begin to show. Direct lines of communication are rerouted through more people and departments. Key objectives become blurred, agendas diverge, and trust slowly dissolves. When this happens, the bread crumbs of almost every problem lead back to insufficient communication, misaligned objectives, or lack of organizational trust.

So how can a company retain its entrepreneurial spirit as it grows? By maintaining CAT.

Addressing the Challenges of Remote Workers

•

It's great that technology enables people to work remotely, but this also presents significant cultural challenges. Remote workers score lower across the board on our employee engagement surveys, and while that's somewhat expected, it's also important to close the gap.

To address this, we bring our remote employees to the corporate office with a cadence that matches the needs of their initiatives. If projects are critical and require collaboration, that generally means monthly. Otherwise, we look at quarterly or twice a year, minimum.

As a business leader, you need to work extra hard to achieve CAT with remote workers. The good news is, the tools exist. From intranets and email to videos, podcasting, and Facebook Live, it's easier than ever to communicate, collaborate, and foster trust with remote workers. It helps quite a bit if you personally live the values of the company. Because with culture, as with your brand, the key isn't technology; it's authenticity.

Communication

Every employee gets a business card at Anytime Fitness, but sometimes we encourage them to throw it out the window. That's our way of saying that most of our communications strategies depend on creating a level playing field in which every person—no matter how high-ranking or how long they've been with us—feels free to speak their mind and offer their opinion. After all, when you weigh in, you buy in.

You'll need to figure out the best way to accomplish this in your organization, but here's a peek at some of the things we've done to improve communication:

- In company meetings, we tell everyone to disregard titles and tenures. It doesn't matter if you've been with us 10 years, 10 months, or 10 days, we want input from every angle of the business. In fact, we intentionally harvest the curiosity and fresh perspectives of new employees, and those employees are often surprised and energized by the engagement they sense from senior leaders on the team.

- We role-play with new employees during the onboarding process, making them say things like, "Dave, I disagree with that idea," or "Chuck, do you have any data to support your decision?" Hey, if you don't practice speaking as an equal, then you're less likely to do it . . .

- We look for opportunities to write all-staff emails, share short videos, and communicate openly at staff events. As a leader, you have to find new ways to get the same message across and drive it home. The bigger the team, the more often you need to reinforce the message.

- We have "Just Ask" boxes around our company headquarters, which allow employees to ask questions and suggest changes anonymously. Yes, this is an analog approach in a digital world, but it works. Recently, an employee challenged us on whether our parental leave policy supported our mission to improve the world's self-esteem. We shared the question in an all-staff email and invited the writer to meet us. Based on those talks, we ended up expanding the policy.

Alignment

"Alignment" can sound like a rigid, top-down term, but it doesn't have to be. We think of it as a pull, not a push. It's not about forcing people to think or behave in a certain way. It's about inspiring them to believe in your mission. And you can do it in creative ways. Amazon founder Jeff Bezos is famous for keeping an empty chair in every meeting to represent the customer. We could mimic that by putting a treadmill in every conference room, but that could get a little cumbersome. Instead, we ask, "How does this benefit our members?" and "How does this benefit the people who invest in owning our gyms?" during every meeting. It's important to keep consumers in mind, but we take it a step further by including all stakeholders in the mix: members, franchise owners, and employees. Frankly, we're surprised how often leaders treat their employees as an afterthought. Our philosophy is "How can we expect our members and franchise owners to love our brand if our employees don't love it first?"

If you want to build a high-performance team, then you need to constantly provide clarity and focus. "Just Do It" might work as a Nike tagline, but it's a terrible mantra for running an organization. People need to know *why* they should do it. They can't fully believe in any given initiative if they don't know the bigger strategy behind it.

One "alignment" tactic that's worked well for us is a tradition of departmental coffee chats. These are quarterly meetings in which entire departments, small groups, or cross-functional teams gather for an open dialogue. We ask people to bring only a pencil, paper, and an open mind. These gatherings are obviously a form of communication, but the result has been a heightened ability to unearth and break down hidden barriers inside the organization, and dramatically improve alignment within individual teams and the company as a whole.

Leaders are too often reluctant to provide transparency to all team members. But people perform better when they have clear visibility of company goals, along with an understanding of why those goals exist in the first place. These types of meetings provide an ideal platform for openly discussing progress toward strategy initiatives. They allow you to identify where more resources or leadership are needed. And the strategic alignment they breed is absolutely critical to achieving high levels of execution.

Trust

Imagine two different companies of roughly the same size. Company A is trust-based; Company B isn't. After an extensive audit, both are presented with some interesting information: While the vast majority of their employees are honest and productive, about 2–3 percent frequently take advantage of current policies. Maybe they consistently come in late and leave early. Maybe they occasionally fudge their expense reports. Maybe they spend half their work time looking at cat videos on social media.

Company B looks at this information and decides to rewrite its employee handbook: From now on, every employee has to punch in and punch out, expense reports must be triple-verified and signed by the CEO, and access to all social media is blocked. By contrast, Company A sees the extremely low noncompliance rate as a sign of a positive culture. It has managers address specific issues with problem employees, but it leaves the policies themselves in place.

By not punishing the many for the sins of the few, Company A is showing that it values the 98 percent more than the 2 percent. Company B, on the other hand, is overreacting. By making policies more onerous for everybody, it's sending the message that the bad eggs have more power than the good eggs—and if that's the case, then why bother being good? In short, Company B values policy over people; Company A values people over policy.

In nearly 30 years of owning businesses of different sizes, we've never had a time clock, never personally tracked an employee's vacation time or PTO, and never verified someone's expense sheet. Have we been taken advantage of? Sure. Have a small percentage of our people violated our trust? Of course. But those are short-term losses, and those employees are never around very long. What's far more important is that we've never lost a great team member because we treated them like an inferior one. When it comes to your organization, trust is both a form of currency and a business multiplier. And in actual practice, if you're strong on Communication and Alignment, Trust is the natural by-product.

The world of franchising presents some unique trust challenges. Your franchisees want you to trust them to run their own businesses, but your customers trust that you'll provide a consistent experience no matter which storefront they walk into. As a result, we've mandated some elements of our business to address customer experience (e.g., giving our gyms a consistent look and feel), while giving our franchisees autonomy in how they grow their businesses. Some stop at owning one gym, others open dozens. And how do the multiple-club owners succeed? By knowing how to identify talent, hire for culture, onboard their people, and empower their teams through a culture of Communication, Alignment, and Trust—just like we do.

Evaluation and Feedback: Beyond the Standard Review

The words "employee review" can often elicit eye rolls among management—as if providing feedback is a necessary evil that interrupts important work. That's unfortunate, because no aspect of leadership packs more power than evaluating and coaching your people.

The good news is that once you've established CAT in your organization, you've already done the heavy lifting. When Communication, Alignment, and Trust achieve an authentic presence in every office, meeting area, and break room, then evaluation and feedback come naturally. In fact, the most effective feedback often happens informally—during coffee chats or while bumping into team members in the hallways. That being said, a formal evaluation process is still a must. As our company has grown, our review process has evolved to fit the needs of a larger business. Yours can and should be unique, but here are some areas we highly recommend covering with your people:

- **Performance.** This should be evaluated from both your perspective and the employee's. Ask the person to identify strengths, weaknesses, achievements, and disappointments since their last review. (Remember what we said about self-awareness?)

- **Personal/professional development and future opportunities.** As with performance, this should be a conversation rather than a review. You should talk with the employee about their personal and professional development plan for their path in the company and in their life. This "walks the walk" in showing that you see them as a person, not just an employee.

- **Update on key objectives.** This is a good time to get a sense of everything the person is involved in at work, as well as any challenges they're facing in their various projects.

- **Cultural values and alignment.** Always use the review process to reinforce the purpose of both the company and the individual, as well as to realign key company strategies and objectives. This is a great opportunity to deliver clarity and focus in a one-on-one setting.

- **Compensation planning.** This is self-explanatory, but it should emerge naturally from the previous topics.

- **Open time for Q&A.** A review should be a conversation, and this part shouldn't be a mere add-on that creates dead air. Make sure the person comes in prepared, and if they have a hard time thinking of questions, ask some yourself.

Investment: The 0.5% Rule

With any asset, you can achieve strong growth only when you reinvest the dividends. That's why we have a formal policy of allocating 0.5 percent of our top-line revenues for employee development. To be clear, these funds aren't exclusive to training directly related to employees' jobs. In keeping with the Level 4 mindset we discussed in Chapter 3, "The 5 Levels of a People-Oriented Work Culture," it applies to personal as well as professional development.

The 0.5% Rule works so well for us that we think it's a great rule of thumb for organizations of any size and type. If your business is running at $400,000 a year, you'll have a $2,000 fund for the year. At $10 million, it'll be $50,000. At $100 million, $500,000. Even if your business is super small—say, $100,000 a year in revenue with few if any full-time employees—$500 can easily fund a seminar, an online learning experience, continuing education credits, or something else that helps develop your most important asset: your people. No investment is too small. And once you get in the habit of executing The 0.5% Rule, it becomes easier to maintain over time.

We strongly believe that only when you maximize these critical touchpoints with your employees—from the first interview to ongoing feedback and development—can you truly build a people-oriented culture. But to test our ideas, we asked a well-known business leader for his unique take.

— CHAPTER 5 —

An Outside Perspective: John Donahoe

"Using coaches and 'consuming help' is a sign of strength, not weakness."

John Donahoe, former president and CEO of eBay and Bain & Company, current chairman of PayPal, and board member of eBay and Intel

John Donahoe has an international reputation as a people-oriented business leader, and he's brought that focus to industries and cultures ranging from online auctions to microchips. Here's what he had to say when we asked for his unique perspective on the virtues of this all-important first P.

What has your experience taught you about valuing people?

Investing in and developing people, helping people achieve their full potential—it's always been part of my wiring. Bain taught me an enormous amount. Professional-services firms are some of the most sophisticated developers of people in the world, because in a sense, human beings are their only asset. And so it's about the ability to systematically develop people—recruiting the right people who are consistent with your culture, helping them build their skills, coaching them, providing constant feedback, and continually challenging them.

I took many of those practices and applied them at eBay. Developing leaders was a very important dimension of what we tried to achieve there, because we're in a world where—especially in technology—organizations are increasingly flat. Everyone's a leader.

What's the key to getting businesses to truly value their people?

At Bain, we had a speaker come in who talked about the "business athlete." He asked everyone in the audience, "How many of you want to be world-class in what you do as a businessperson?" Everyone raised their hand. He said, "Okay, let's look at world-class athletes. For every hour they're on the playing field, they probably put in 20 hours of preparation. World-class athletes are very clear about their strengths and weaknesses. They train to leverage their strengths and augment their weaknesses by working on them. World-class athletes use coaches.

The point is that using coaches and "consuming help" is a sign of strength, not weakness. When Michael Jordan came onto the basketball scene, he had a chef. He had a lifting coach, a mental coach. He had multiple conditioning coaches. He invested in his mental and emotional well-being. Coaching isn't a soft, fuzzy thing. It's about being able to perform.

The speaker said, "You know, I don't get you guys in business. You expect to be world-class by always being on the playing field. You know all the answers all the time. You act like you're Superman—like you don't need to sleep, you don't need to eat well, you don't need to work out. If you really want to be world-class, how are you going to do it if you haven't trained, prepared yourself, and taken care of yourself?"

How did that perspective affect you?

It made the light bulb go off for me at a very early stage in my career. I remember thinking, "Wait, getting help and investing in myself isn't a sign of weakness?" No, it was the exact opposite. It was the smartest thing you could do. So when I need to perform on the playing field—in business or in life—I'm more prepared. That little bit of a reframing made me an aggressive consumer of all kinds of coaches: peers, mentors, couples' groups, priests, Buddhists. It's a wide variety of people, but it's all about "How do I develop my full capacity so that when I get to play this wonderful game called 'life' or 'business,' I'm as prepared as I can be?" Because, by the way, it's hard! That's the other learning. Accomplishing anything great is hard. And it never looks pretty in the moment.

You're a big sports fan. What do sports teach us about people and how to better perform as individuals and teams?

I love sports because I love watching world-class athletes, and world-class athletes know the difference between being #1 and being #2. Take the World Cup. It takes two years of preparation to get down to the best two teams in the world, and do you know what the final scores of the last three World Cup Finals have been? 1–0, 1–0, and 1–1 (with a victory on penalty kicks). After two years of intense competition, the difference between being #1 and #2 is often just one goal. And World Cup games are ugly. You get muddy, you get injured—and by the way, in the last World Cup final, the best player for Germany got hurt in the first half. And the guy who scored the winning goal was his substitute. In a way, that tells you everything you need to know.

The difference between being #1, which everyone remembers, and #2, which no one remembers, is tiny, but also huge. This notion of "I expect it to be easy, and I expect to get positive feedback along the way"—it's just crazy. It's not that way in sports, and it's not that way in business.

Moving to Action: People
with Carol Grannis, Ed.D.

All you need is a journal, some uninterrupted time (30 minutes will do), and some vulnerability. Here are some exercises to get you moving forward in the area of people.

•

Carol Grannis, Ed.D., Chief Self Esteem Officer for SEB

5 Things You Can Do Right Now

1. Look at the "5 Levels of a People-Oriented Work Culture" (Chapter 3) and determine which level best applies to your organization right now.

2. Write down five things you can do to help move yourself to the next level.

3. Write out your current hiring process and see how it matches up with the process Chuck and Dave outlined in Chapter 4, "Designing a People Culture."

4. Do the same for your onboarding process and see how it matches up with the Onboarding Checklist that Chuck and Dave provided.

5. Based on John Donahoe's advice about "consuming help," write down three areas in which you will seek out coaching or mentorship in the next month—because it all starts with you.

Big Ideas in This Section

Show some love. The focus of this section is about how you feel about and behave with the people who work for and with you. An emphasis on people means that you're caring for your employees, valuing their perspective, and trusting that their intentions for you and the success of your business are good. And the trust is reciprocal: They trust that your intentions for their success are high. When you have an emphasis on people, you know about their lives and you support their life events.

Wax on, wax off. A focus on people means that you invest in their development and learning. And if someone makes a mistake, you use that as a learning opportunity. Leaders who have a focus on people are great coaches. They find opportunities to focus on their employees through scheduled and informal meetings. They're truly present, and they really listen.

With a little help from your friends. Leaders who have a focus on people support collaboration and teams. They want people working together, learning from each other, and working toward common goals.

Welcome aboard. Lastly, this section focuses on the tangible activities of making sure you're welcoming the right people onto your team—through hiring, onboarding, and providing ongoing feedback on how they're doing.

Journaling Exercises

For the following mental exercises, take out a journal, turn off your phone, and write in longhand (if you still remember how).

"One by One"

- Write down the first name of everyone who works directly for you.
- Think about your relationship with each person.
- Rate each relationship on a scale of 1–10 (1: You're not

even sure what their last name is; 10: You're proud of how you value this person and you show it).

Now answer these questions:

- What impact does this current relationship have on you, the employee, other team members, and customers?

- What would happen if you did nothing to improve any of these numbers?

- Which relationship had the highest number and how did it get there?

- Which relationship had the lowest number and how did it get there?

"Develop Much?"

- Think about your current practice of development and training for your employees.

- Estimate how much time, money, or other resources you invest with your employees currently.

Now answer these questions:

- Which of your employees has received the most development/training?

- Is there a correlation with the rating you gave that employee regarding your relationship and the amount of training they have received?

- Which training or development practices are working

well, and how do they benefit your customers?

- What are some options to training and development you could implement that would add the most value to your business?

Online Resources @ www.PeoplePurposeProfitsPlay.com

The process of building a skill begins by being intentional and focused on what you want to get better at or develop. Here are some online tools that can help you create some habits that will have a powerful impact on your focus on people.

- Building Trust: River of Life,[7] Personal Histories, and 36 Questions

- Hiring: Job Descriptions and Interview Guides

- Onboarding: 90-Day Plan and FastStart Tools

- Training: Development Planning Tools and 9 Block

- Teams: Team Meeting Checklist and Drawing People Out

A Story to Tell: Rachele Jordan

Rachele Jordan, Anytime Fitness C2i (Coach to Inspire)

Early in 2012, Chuck and Dave had each Anytime Fitness employee write down their three top "bucket list" items, but they didn't say why. I had always wanted to take my sons to Australia to meet their Aussie family members. But as a single mom, it wasn't something I could afford on my own. So that's what I wrote down as my #1 wish.

Over the course of that year, a dozen or so people won something called the Peer-to-Peer PLEASE Award for exemplary customer service, and I was one of them. At our annual holiday party, Chuck and Dave invited all the winners onstage to read their bucket lists. Most of us, including me, were overcome with emotion as we revisited those items.

Chuck and Dave then announced that all the lists were going into a hat, and whoever's name was drawn randomly would get their top wish granted. As luck would have it, mine wasn't drawn, but Chuck and Dave were apparently so moved by my list that they granted my wish as well!

The trip was a dream come true. We went up the Queensland coast and saw my family, and my sons suddenly understood Australia beyond their mom's funny accent and kooky sayings. I still hear them brag about the country to their friends. They tell great stories and remember the smallest details about each of my family members. And they now empathize more with the fact that since I live in the American Midwest, I don't get to see these loved ones very often.

The whole experience deepened my relationship with my sons. I think of it almost every day, and that amazing gesture has provided a level of trust and gratitude that makes work feel like anything but work.

Because my work valued people, the people in my immediate and extended families became closer. That's a gift you can't put a price on, and one that I'll never forget.

A Story to Tell: "The Planking Grandma"

Betty Lou Sweeney, Anytime Fitness member

We alluded to Betty Lou Sweeney at the beginning of this section, and here's the whole amazing tale of her life. Betty Lou is too shy to tell her own story, so we're doing it for her (with her permission, of course), because she's one of the most amazing people you'll ever meet. In a way, her story tells you everything you need to know about people, perseverance, and how to achieve success.

Betty Lou spent most of her adult life overweight. Already a bit shy, her physical appearance further siphoned her confidence and suppressed her personality. At the age of 50, she joined a local fitness center in hopes of getting in better shape. Unfortunately, she was ignored by the club staff. Within weeks of joining, she quit and went right back to her unhealthy ways.

Two decades years later, Betty Lou found herself 110 pounds overweight and taking 25 medications a day for health problems, mostly related to her obesity. She decided to give fitness one more chance by joining an Anytime Fitness that had opened in her small Wisconsin town. This time, her gym experience was different. The staff was friendly, and the equipment was top quality. But the doors to a healthier place really opened up when she met Dave Candra.

Dave was a recently certified personal trainer in his early 20s, and Betty had no idea that at the time they met, he seriously doubted his ability to make any money doing what he loved. In fact, Betty Lou was Dave's first real client. But from their first training session, this duo—separated by nearly 50 years—had an instant chemistry. Over the next two years, Betty went on to lose 110 pounds. At 71, she now takes just one medication a day.

If the story ended here, it would still be great. But that's just the half of it.

During their training work, Dave and Betty Lou made an amazing discovery: Betty Lou had a superhuman talent for planking. Planking is a serious core workout in which you place your forearms on the ground and rise up on your toes until your body is in a straight line from feet to head. Betty Lou was able *to hold a plank so long, she was approaching the world record of 30 minutes.[8] Catching wind of this, Anytime Fitness invited her to the Mall of America to go for the record in public. She barely slept a wink before the event, and during her attempt in front of a huge audience and three local television crews, she failed at around the 10-minute mark. She was disappointed, but not embarrassed. The steely look in her eyes said, "This isn't the last you'll see of me."*

A week later—this time in the comfort of her Anytime Fitness club in Steven's Point, Wisconsin—Betty Lou set the world record for planking at 36 minutes and 58 seconds. That record has since been broken, but it's still a stunning achievement, especially for a grandmother who used to be in such poor health.

Betty Lou's emotional change has been even more remarkable. With newfound confidence and energy, she's a ball of energy. And now she's using that energy to work as a personal trainer herself.

---

[7] River of Life is a visual narrative method that helps people tell stories of the past, present, and future.

[8] For the record, Chuck and Dave tap out at about three minutes.

— **PART II** —

Purpose

> "The promise of a big payday isn't enough of a motivator. People crave fulfillment and purpose in their work, and most want to be a part of something that makes an impact beyond them."
>
> —David Horsager, best-selling author of *The Trust Edge*

Formative Purpose Moment

•

When I was growing up, a 60-year-old widow lived next door to us. Because she lived alone, my parents would make me shovel not only her sidewalk but also her stairs, the pathway from her house to the street, the house to the garage, and driveway into the garage. It was a big job for a 10-year-old, and I swear Minnesota winters were a lot worse back then.

I whined about it at first, but after a few times seeing her walk on a clean, safe sidewalk, it became a sense of pride. A weird thing happened where I actually started looking forward to shoveling for her, and eventually I started putting more effort into her walk than our own.

It took time and sweat, but it left me feeling purposeful, and I still remember those feelings today.

—Chuck

W e both remember the moment. It was August 2005, and we were standing in front of 130 people, eyes watering, two 50-lb. dumbbells lodged in our throats. To our right, Anytime Fitness member Pat Welsh was reading a speech, hands trembling, as his wife sat sobbing in the front row. It was the biggest community blubber fest we'd ever seen, with not a dry eye among the Anytime Fitness gym owners in the room.

This was our first annual conference in August 2005. Today these events are held in different locations each year and draw upward of 3,000 people from all over the world. But in 2005, we were just a small group of mostly local folks. Pat was a member from Hibbing, Minnesota, and for most of his life, he had struggled with not only his weight but also the burdens that come with an unhealthy lifestyle. His self-esteem and energy were low, and he didn't like how he looked or felt. Previous efforts at change had failed, but Pat gave himself one more chance when he joined our gym. This time he hired a personal trainer. And together they helped Pat lose over 100 lbs. in under a year.

Pat was speaking because he and two others had just received our first-ever "Member Success Story Award." In his speech, Pat thanked his wife and his personal trainer for their support. But the most poignant moment came when he described his new life versus his old life. He felt pride in his accomplishments, but he also feared that he might slip back into his unhealthy ways. While he was hopeful and energized for his future, you could also sense his regret at having lost so many years to inaction and negative thoughts.

Seeing the faces in the audience that night was an indelible moment for us, because Pat's speech obviously hit home with our club owners and trainers in a deep way. These people were witnesses to the daily struggles of others, and Pat's speech reminded us that health is emotional terrain. Out of those collective tears came the first spark of a passionate fire of purpose that still burns hot within Anytime Fitness today. We would start many new traditions after that night. Most important, we would begin to produce and share emotional videos of Member Success Stories like Pat's at every conference. To this day, these stories never fail to put that big lump back in our throat.

Purpose is the impact your organization has beyond economic or personal gain. It's something your people feel in their head, heart, and gut. In short, it's what gets them out of bed in the morning, energizes them throughout the day, and keeps them coming back for more.

In this P (Purpose) section:

- We'll tackle how to find purpose both in yourself and in your organization—regardless of your size or industry.

- We'll look at how Anytime Fitness has built a tattoo-worthy brand that rivals companies like Harley-Davidson.

- We'll share a valuable outside perspective from a leader whose company has instilled a strong sense of purpose in an industry not necessarily known for it.

— CHAPTER 6 —

Purpose Starts with You

> "Everyone can help.
> Get off the sidelines."
>
> —Slogan of the Oklahoma Youth Wrestling Foundation

It was the summer of 2011, and we were sequestered in a run-down house in an impoverished Oklahoma City neighborhood called Central Park. Outside, it was 95 degrees and humid. Inside, it was even worse. We had no air conditioning and no TV, radio, phones, or newspapers. For one week, we had agreed to be cut off from our homes, our families, and our comforts. As we sat on a ratty couch contemplating how we were going to survive on $71 for 6 days, a parade of roaches, spiders, and millipedes crawled past our feet.

This was the shoot for *Secret Millionaire*, the ABC show designed to give CEO types a dose of reality while they volunteer for local charities. We had agreed to do the show thinking that we could help out some worthwhile causes. We had no idea how much the experience would help us.

Based on the lifestyles we have now, Oklahoma City was a jolt to the system. During the day, we volunteered for several micro-charities that we would eventually write checks to, including the Oklahoma Youth Wrestling Foundation (educating at-risk youth through wrestling), Limbs for Life (free prosthetic limbs for kids and adults in need), and Closer to Earth (creating positive action for youth through organic gardening, landscaping, and composting). Every night, we returned to our stuffy little house with nothing to do except talk—which had an interesting way of conjuring stories from the past. Like Limbs for Life customers who experience the "phantom pain" of limbs they've lost, we sometimes found ourselves recalling some of the more painful moments from our childhoods.

For Dave, memories of his hardscrabble youth came flooding back. Being the youngest of multiple siblings—with a dad who was always driving a truck and a mom who worked night shifts—he often found himself alone in a way that the OKC wrestlers could probably relate to. For Chuck, the week revived memories of a lost brother. Steve Runyon was born with a hole in his heart, and even though he lived 13 years longer than his prognosis, he eventually died on the operating table—a life cut short at just 18.

Talking about and reliving these experiences brought more than a few tears to that Oklahoma City couch, but the experience had another effect on us that might seem superficial at first. Right away, we had noticed how the lawn in front of our house, and those of most of the neighborhood, were overgrown and neglected. That's a nice way of saying it. They looked like shit. And it made us wonder: What makes a person care or not care about their lawn, and how does that decision impact an entire neighborhood over time?

This lawn situation wasn't unlike our business, where for years we had seen some gym owners maintain spotless spaces while others let trash cans overflow and ignored the ripped upholstery on their weight machines. We knew from experience that how a gym owner treated their club directly influenced how their members treated it as well. And we had long preached the idea that caring and apathy were equally contagious qualities.

With that in mind, we decided that instead of trying to relax between our volunteering stints, we would take ownership of our house and our situation. The TV crew, which usually sat comfortably in their air-conditioned van, scrambled to grab their cameras the first time they saw us emerge from the house and start pulling weeds. Dave talked a neighbor into letting us use his mower for a $5 tip (7 percent of our food budget), and we gave everything a good trim.

It wasn't exactly Augusta National when we were finished, but it was a big improvement. As a final touch at the end of the week, we reinstalled the board with the home's address on it (1203) as a way of saying, "This house mattered. We were here. And hopefully we made it better." Without really thinking about it, we made a small gesture to get the community to a healthier place.

The simple act of improving our lawn had nothing to do with the charities or the show. Not much of it made the final cut when our episode finally aired on ABC. But it had everything to do with who we wanted to be and what we wanted to stand for. The experience inspired us to recommit ourselves to always being in the "care" versus "apathy" category, and encouraging others to join us.

When Dave returned to Oklahoma City a few months later, he ventured back to the neighborhood we lived in, and guess what? Every lawn was mowed. We can't prove that we started the movement, but frankly, there's no other good explanation for it. One house cared, so others followed. It's not that complicated when you think about it.

Look in the Purpose Mirror

As *Secret Millionaire* and Oklahoma City reminded us, purpose truly does start at the top—with leadership, with *your* actions. Think of the job you had growing up that was the most monotonous. How did it make you feel? Chuck was once a security guard with nothing to actually guard. Maybe some people would love the chance to collect a paycheck for doing basically nothing, but he hated it. Why? Because there was no stimulation, no *purpose*. And if you don't have an authentic passion for your business, you and the business will never perform at a high level.

Anytime Fitness was already a purpose-based organization in 2011, but our time in Oklahoma City kicked us into another gear. Many elements contributed to that, but part of it was the fact that we spent the entire week shoulder-to-shoulder with everyday people who put their time, money, heart, and soul into making their organizations work and making people's lives better. For example, we met Tyler and Shelby at the OKC Youth Wrestling Foundation—two humble guys who are absolute superheroes to the kids who wrestle, exercise, read, eat a good meal, and find community in their gym. We met Amy and Pam at Limbs for Life, who spend every day helping people walk, run, and live normal lives instead of feeling "disabled." Is there a more important mission than that? And we met Allen Parleir and the teen staff at Closer to Earth.

As a leader, there's no "one size fits all" when it comes to purpose, and you don't have to sleep among the cockroaches to figure it out. In fact, *Secret Millionaire* made us realize that even though we're both purpose-based leaders, we arrive at purpose in very different ways. Dave takes things in through his heart. He feels something first, then it travels up to his brain so he can think about it. Chuck is more cerebral. He thinks first, then feels. We're opposites in that way, but (lucky for us) our approaches complement each other.

After *Secret Millionaire*, we decided to honor that insight by using the terms "heartfirst" and "brainfirst" to describe ourselves and others. The important thing is to realize that there's no judgment attached to those words. Someone who's brainfirst isn't necessarily smarter, and someone who's heartfirst doesn't necessarily care more. But knowing where you fall on that spectrum as a leader can help you better understand how you see the world and what issues you're most passionate about.

When you look in your purpose mirror, what do you see? What do you truly care about that's bigger than you? When you look at the landscape of charitable organizations and causes, which ones resonate with you? Most important, what are you going to do about it?

Get in the Game

At the beginning of this chapter, we quoted the slogan of the OKC Youth Wrestling Foundation. Those four words—"get off the sidelines"—serve as a good reminder for business leaders of all kinds. It's one thing to talk about purpose. It's another to walk the walk.

At the end of our time in Oklahoma City, we donated nearly $500,000 to the organizations we interacted with. We would have done that regardless, but it was also an expected part of the *Secret Millionaire* show. The bigger question was: How would the experience affect us once we got back home to Minnesota?

We were already personally involved in plenty of good causes, and so were many of our employees and franchisees. But we decided that it was time to take the next step at Anytime Fitness, so we started the HeartFirst Charitable Foundation™. This organization is made possible in part by the generosity of our franchise network. Participating clubs contribute $100 per month to the Foundation and receive access to marketing materials promoting their involvement in the program, both in their clubs and in their communities.

HeartFirst has proved to be a great way to operationalize purpose and pair good deeds with good business. Our first recipients were Hannah and Tristan Ambrozewski, two Army vets motivated to serve their country after 9/11. After meeting in training camp, they became intelligence analysts in Iraq, then eventually married and started a family. Now, thanks to HeartFirst, they own an Anytime Fitness gym near Fort Bragg in Fayetteville, North Carolina, where they employ fellow veterans while getting their members to a healthier place.

We'll talk more about how to infuse purpose into your organization in the next chapter, "Building a Tattoo-Worthy Brand." But the bottom line is, it starts at the top. You lead your brand, not the other way around. If people see you living an authentic purpose in your own life, then they'll be inspired to take action as well. So when it comes to purpose, leaders need to get in the game.

HeartFirst recipients Hannah and Tristan Ambrozewski

— CHAPTER 7 —

Building a Tattoo-Worthy Brand

"64% of millennials would rather earn $40,000 a year at a job they love than $100,000 a year at a job they find unfulfilling."

—The Intelligence Group

In the never-ending "Beatles vs. Stones" battle, Chuck is more of a Stones guy, while Dave favors The Beatles. Why do we mention this? Because we're going to start this chapter in an unlikely place: music.

How do you explain our universal emotional connection with music? You can't, really. It's completely subjective and impossible to quantify with data. Our tastes are influenced by the era we grew up in, our friends, and the discovery of a melody, musician, or lyrics that align with life's most significant people and moments. Our iTunes playlists are probably as unique as our fingerprints. Yet everybody likes music on some level. It can crank up our energy or soothe our souls, and it alone has the power to make us dance, sing, laugh, cry, and transform ourselves into air-guitar-playing idiots.

Most important, when we discover a band we like, what do we do? We start to think of them as *ours*. We download their songs, share them with friends, go to their concerts, and buy their T-shirts. The music we love becomes a part of us. And if we're truly fanatical, we might even get a tattoo of a band's logo in a prominent or discreet location.

Can being at work be like being in a band? It sounds like an absurd comparison, but why not? They're both collaborative processes in which people blend their talents to produce something to share with the world. If enough people like the product, it can be monetized through various channels of commerce. And like a band, your company can metaphorically move from playing coffee shops and small clubs to headlining sports arenas and major outdoor festivals.

But for any of this to happen, you have to do two things: Speak to the heart, and speak *from* the heart. When Anytime Fitness member Pat Welsh gave his heartfelt speech at our first conference about how our company had saved his life, another remarkable thing happened later that night: Mike Gelfgot, a Russian immigrant and Anytime Fitness franchise owner, became such a fan of our purpose that he went out and got a tattoo of our "Runningman" logo on his left arm.

Now that we know Mike better, it's not surprising that he was the first person to do this. After visiting him dozens of times over the years, we've never seen him have a low-energy day. He's a heartfirst guy who feels his way through life, and everyone who meets him can instantly feel his passion for helping others. But back in 2005, no one (including us) suspected that Mike's literal "branding" of Anytime Fitness would go viral.

Today, more than 3,000 Anytime Fitness fans and band members—including our employees, franchisees, members, vendors, personal trainers, and yes, founders—now sport Runningman tattoos. These aren't just crazy Americans. The group also includes people from Canada, Mexico, Chile, the UK, India, Japan, Australia, and Qatar. Each person customizes their tattoo, and like an iTunes playlist, no two are quite the same.

Our company tattoo parlor

LOVE WORK

Chuck showing off his tattoo—and his son, Charlie

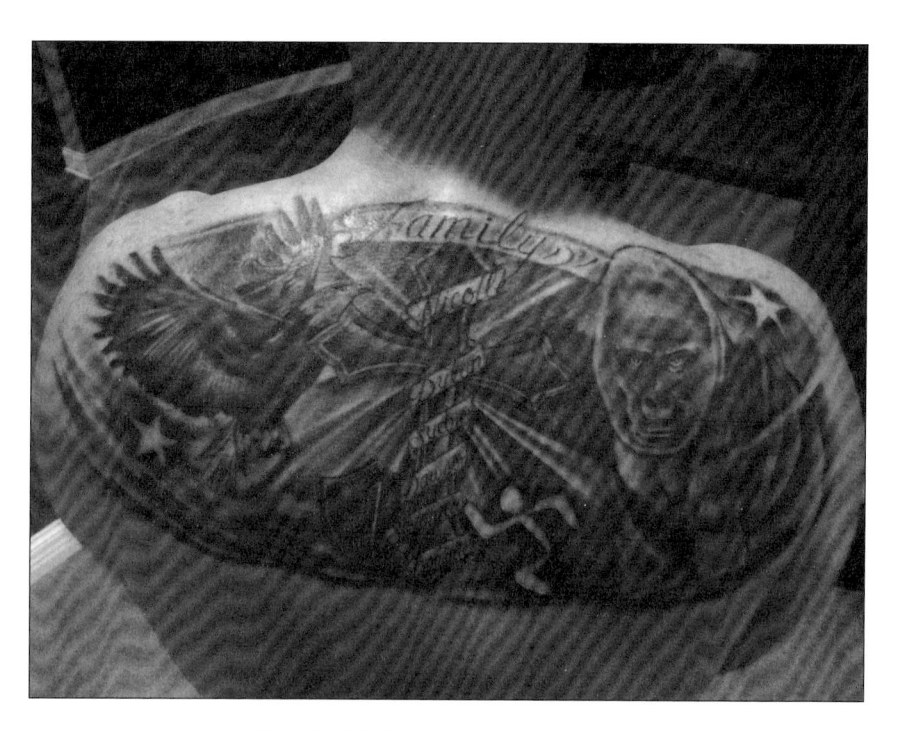

Dave's slightly more aggressive tattoo

Passion Comes in Many Forms

Outsiders are always fascinated to learn about Anytime Fitness's tattoo fandom, because it's highly unusual for a corporate brand (other than Harley-Davidson) to elicit this kind of passion. Some people even view it with a dose of cynicism. When someone asked Anytime Fitness member Levi Landry why in the world he had a Runningman tattoo on his calf, he looked them straight in the eye and said, "Two and half years ago, I was in a car accident that killed my wife and kids, and frankly, the only thing that keeps me alive is coming to this gym." Enough said.

We actually do know why most people get Anytime Fitness tattoos, because we reimburse anyone who gets one, so long as they tell us why they did it. Each reason is unique, but there's a pattern: No one has ever inked themselves with our logo because they thought we had the best treadmills, because we're open 24/7, because we offer good benefits, because they saved money during a membership sale, or because they've managed to make a good living by operating one of our gyms. Instead, their "whys" fall into two main categories. For some, the tattoo is a symbol of the person we helped them discover inside themselves. For others, it honors a person that they helped transform.

In the first category, you can hear the echoes of Pat Welsh. Our members talk about how they've fallen in love with their new self, and how their tattoo is a symbol of greater self-respect. This is critically important, because as one of our success story subjects put it a few years ago, "You can't fully love others unless you love yourself first."

These tattoo stories are always deeply personal, and most describe a major physical and emotional transformation.

We've heard our share of weight-loss stories, and these are always impressive. But it runs far deeper than that. We've heard members describe how they overcame eating disorders, depression, and addiction. We've heard wounded warriors tell us that our people helped them cope with or overcome post-traumatic stress. We've read how it felt when someone completed their first 5K or marathon, performed in their first fitness show, or finally became the role model for their kids that they always wanted to be.

Von Hollingsworth and Anna Dey provide a great example. As a father-daughter team who own an Anytime Fitness club near Cleveland, they're as serious about running a profitable business as they are about changing lives, and it shows. They started their Anytime Fitness franchise in 2012, at the ages of 54 and 24, after deciding to make fitness a priority in their lives. In terms of business performance and community engagement, their gym is among our highest-performing clubs. And they've raised over $100,000 for their local community, most recently collecting over $30,000 for three children with cancer.

Von and Anna both have Anytime Fitness tattoos. Even better, 22 of their members have gone under the purple needle (and counting), and all the tattoos pictured in this chapter come from their members. But Von and Anna's passion doesn't stop there. A few years ago, Anna married her sweetheart, Mike Dey. Rather than have a traditional ceremony, they climbed Mt. Kilimanjaro and got hitched at the summit. And guess what? They celebrated with a purple Anytime Fitness flag.

This was completely unsolicited, and it's not the only

time our brand has appeared at the top of mountains. We've had franchise owners and members raise our flag not only at Kilimanjaro but also at Mount Rainier, Machu Picchu, and the base camp of Mount Everest. Photos have come to us of people scuba diving, skydiving, and sailing with our flag in some of the world's most gorgeous places. These images are like tattoos of their own, and for the record, we've never seen the flags of other franchises proudly displayed on mountains, shaved heads, ocean floors, or body parts. Do these businesses make money? Sure, and that money pays bills and allows you to purchase stuff. But we see purpose as a type of "currency for the soul" that buys indelible experiences and a meaningful life.

"Anytime Fitness is my happy place. The trainers and members make this place another family."
—Kaci Fuller

LOVE WORK

"Anytime Fitness really is a family. My tattoo represents this family and a decision to live my life to the fullest."
—Steve Pustay

"Becoming a member and then being hired as a personal trainer has been so enriching to my life. Helping other people get to a healthier place is what I'm meant to do at this point in my life."
—Lisa Courtney

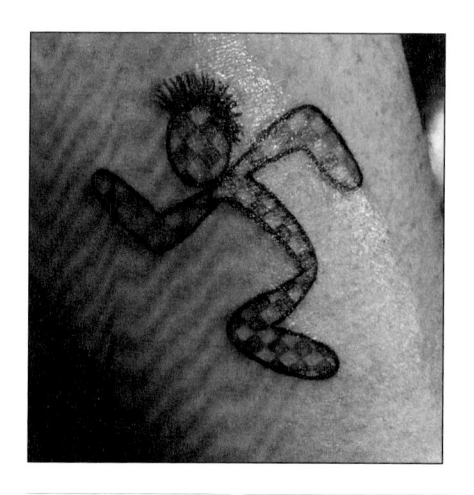

"I'm a Croatian contemporary punk, and my tattoo shows my heritage and lifestyle."
—Dave Horvat

Building a Tattoo-Worthy Brand

Anna and Mike Dey

Anytime Fitness gym owner Mark Stevens (Tupelo, Mississippi) and member Travis Hunsicker

LOVE WORK

Anytime Fitness member Jerry McNeil, atop a summit adjacent to Mount Everest, on his 70th birthday.

Anytime Fitness franchisee Chad Aaron and his son, Colin

The second major reason that people get our tattoo points to the fact that for most human beings, the path to self-improvement—like the path to the top of a mountain—isn't easy. Nor is it ever done completely alone. That's why the logo of our umbrella company, Self Esteem Brands, features a mountain. And that's why our owners and trainers see themselves as Sherpas whose mission is to help people climb the steep path to better health.

Like the story of "Planking Grandma" Betty Lou Sweeney and her trainer, Dave Candra, for every Anytime Fitness member who has changed their life, there's an invaluable person who has guided them along the way. Our member success stories are filled with tales of club owners who take members in and treat them with respect and dignity, as well as personal trainers who listen carefully to members' goals and offer the kind of empathy, support, and tough love they haven't found anywhere else. These "helpers" get their tattoos to commemorate the impact they've had on other people. Because if you change one person's life, it changes yours as well.

"But What If We Sell Widgets?"

We've talked about purpose for many years—sometimes in front of large crowds at conferences other than our own—and we often hear a common question from people in the audience. "Being purpose-based is easy for you guys; you're in the health industry," they say. "But our industry doesn't lend itself to purpose, so what do we do?"

It's a fair point, and we'd be lying if we said that purpose isn't slightly easier to instill in your culture when you work in fitness versus selling envelopes, for example. But even for us, finding our authentic mission in life wasn't automatic. Our industry is littered with businesses that care more about lifting their account balances than lifting people out of obesity, diabetes, or depression. In fact, it's no secret that some big-box gyms stake their profitability on hoping that most of their members *don't* show up at the gym—which is a depressing thought.

A quote often attributed to Maya Angelou states that people will forget what you said and what you did, but they'll never forget how you made them feel. No matter what you sell on paper, ask yourself, "What do we *really* sell? How do we make people *feel*?" We didn't know right away that we were in the business of changing lives, making people feel better about themselves, and raising the world's self-esteem. It took us years to figure that out. If your business isn't naturally wired with purpose, that certainly doesn't prevent you from bringing a sense of purpose into your organization. Here are four ways to get started.

1. **"George Bailey" yourself.**

    Most of us have seen the classic holiday movie *It's a Wonderful Life*, where George Bailey (Jimmy Stewart) gets a chance to see the impact he's made on others by experiencing a life in which he'd never been born. One way to find purpose in your organization is to "George Bailey" your company: Look inward and ask yourself: What would happen if we didn't exist? Who would it impact, and how?

If your company had never even started, where would your employees be working today? How would their families be doing? How many memories would be lost? How many Christmas presents would never be given, college tuition payments never paid, family trips never taken?

Let people convey how their job impacted them and their families, and how their co-workers have influenced their life. Bring those stories to life by sharing them at staff meetings, making videos, sharing them in all-staff emails, or publishing them on your company intranet. It's an eye-opening exercise. And when you do it, chances are you'll unearth a surprising number of heartwarming and inspirational stories.

2. **"BASF" yourself.**

Those of you of a certain age will remember those famous commercials from the '90s that went: "We don't make the plane; we make it lighter. We don't make the lotion; we make it smoother. We don't make the dress; we make it brighter. We don't make the carpet; we make it tougher. At BASF, we don't make a lot of the products you buy; we make a lot of the products you buy better."

These ads were so effective because they took things that were mundane (BASF dealt in chemicals and plastics) and made them relevant, important, and even sexy. As you heard the words, you were also hit with highly emotional images in slow motion: parents lifting babies, kids playing hockey in the living room, an attractive woman modeling a dress. Even if you had no idea what BASF really did, you walked away associating the company with "making life better." And that was the whole point.

Some franchises, including gyms, want their buildings to be high-level customer destinations. For example, Howard Schultz has stated that he wants Starbucks to be your "third place" (along with home and work). We admire that ambition, but in our case, we don't think your third place should be a gym; it should be gardening, camping, golfing, fishing, or whatever hobbies or activities make you the happiest.

Anytime Fitness doesn't seek to be your third place; we want to make all your other places better by giving you more strength and energy. That's our BASF, and this is exactly the process you need to go through as a leader. How does your product or service make things better? Coca-Cola is essentially nothing but carbonated sugar water. But because it's so universally enjoyed, it has associated itself with "bringing the world together." Nike was originally just another athletic shoe, but its long-running "Just Do It" campaign has made it synonymous with grit and determination.

If you sell envelopes, think big about people and the planet. How has the simple, time-honored act of mailing a letter connected people, places, and cultures across time? Do you really sell envelopes, or do you sell connection? Every organization has a broader impact. Whatever you do, don't underestimate it. Honor it.

3. **"Cause" yourself.**

Third, consider adopting a cause. Even if there's no direct line between your products and a charity, you can still find a mission that feels relevant to your culture, and then put company resources behind it in the form of contributions, volunteerism, or mentoring.

No matter what you sell, it's never been easier to find a cause to care about. McDonald's has long funded the Ronald McDonald house, a sanctuary for families dealing with long hospital stays. During Starbucks' 2008 Leadership Conference, 10,000 employees spent the day performing community service to help residents dealing with the effects of Hurricane Katrina. Nike supports the Girl Effect, a non-profit initiative to provide better opportunities for young girls in challenging communities. And the list goes on.

Keep in mind: Having a purpose isn't just for big companies or big charities. In fact, during our *Secret Millionaire* experience, one of our takeaways was just how many micro-charities exist in every community. Some of these organizations operate with annual budgets of less than $50,000, so every dollar or hour of volunteer work makes a huge difference. Hundreds of charitable opportunities probably exist within your region, so it's not hard to find a cause you can support.

In Chapter 8, you'll read about Bell Bank's "Pay It Forward" program, and in Chapter 12, you'll learn about Salesforce's "Pledge 1%" movement. Both provide great examples of companies that have found ways to institute a deep sense of purpose within their cultures, even though what they sell—software and banking services—doesn't immediately lend itself to purpose. These companies don't make these efforts simply because they're led by nice people (although they are). Their purpose-based efforts empower them to offer a more attractive value proposition, attract and retain more talented people, achieve higher engagement, reduce the costs of turnover, and fuel growth. Even better: They can differentiate themselves in the eyes of their customers, and enrich their communities far beyond economic gain.

4. **501(c)(3) yourself.**

Many organizations operationalize their purpose by setting up a separate foundation or charitable arm, also known as a 501(c)(3). This is fairly easy for large corporations to do. But if you're a small to midsize business, it can be a tedious, time-consuming, and burdensome process filled with regulatory hoops. We know this from personal experience.

Years ago, we wanted to start an organization called "Operation Heartfirst." Many military veterans face incredible difficulties with emotional detachment, unemployment, and feeling as though they've lost their purpose when they return from active duty. So our goal was to support military veterans with grants and scholarships to open their own Anytime Fitness gyms, and hopefully employ fellow veterans or family members.

As we embarked on setting up a 501(c)(3) organization, however, we soon experienced the onerous realities of running your own charity while also trying to manage a fast-growing global business. We'll spare you the bureaucratic details, but suffice it to say, a charity can't be run effectively as a hobby or side project. We knew that our first priority was supporting our network of franchise owners. But as entrepreneurs, we also didn't want to give up on the idea of Operation HeartFirst.

Luckily, we found a middle ground. After researching groups that support military veterans, we found one right in our own backyard. Tee It Up for the Troops uses golf as a fundraising and social activity to support and connect the veteran community. So we joined forces. They use their existing operations to collect, disburse, and report funds to meet the regulatory scrutiny under IRS guidelines for a 501(c)(3). We use our business for awareness, fundraising, and locating markets and sites for veteran-owned Anytime Fitness clubs. This partnership has bolstered both of our efforts—and allowed us to support a great cause without losing focus on our business.

No matter how big or small your organization is, you probably have partnership opportunities you didn't even know existed. And remember, charities don't just need money. They value volunteering, donated goods, and in-kind services to help them run. Your expertise in marketing, technology, legal, or accounting services may help them run a more impactful organization. And by helping them fulfill their purpose, you'll also fulfill your own.

Your Purpose-Based Call to Action

Purpose mixes brainpower with heartpower to engage leaders and employees at a higher level. And when a team is engaged, they produce better outcomes. We all have an internal ledger that's adding or subtracting from a life of impact and legacy. Being part of something bigger than ourselves is a currency for the soul. It's deposited in feelings of happiness, satisfaction, and helping others—and we spend it in gratitude, love, and self-respect.

Purpose makes us climb mountains, both real and metaphorical. It spurs us to volunteer or work extra hours to raise money for people and organizations in need; to live for Mondays like other people live for weekends; to not need an alarm clock; and to believe in something so deeply that it leaves an internal tattoo on our heart, mind, and soul.

The purpose-based life is a life even more worth living. So act on it today, both individually and as an organization. You won't regret it—just like our next interview guest.

— CHAPTER 8 —

An Outside Perspective: Michael Solberg

"Giving profoundly impacts us, the givers, as much as those who receive the donations."

Michael Solberg, Bell Bank president & CEO

When it comes to operationalizing purpose, nobody does it better than Mike Solberg, president and CEO of Bell Bank. With assets of over $4 billion and business in 50 states, Bell Bank is the largest independently owned bank in the upper Midwest. And the company attributes a great deal of its success to a program that has nothing to do with investments or interest rates: Pay It Forward.

Your Pay It Forward program really drives home a personal way to engage your employees in the gift of giving. How would you describe the program for someone who doesn't know about it?

Through Pay It Forward, every full-time employee receives $1,000 and every part-timer $500 each year to give away as they choose to individuals, families, or organizations in need. To date, we've empowered more than $10 million in grassroots giving through this program.

Where did the idea for Pay It Forward come from, and when did it start?

My wife, Charleen, and I came up with the idea based on Oprah Winfrey's Pay It Forward challenge. We refined the concept and announced Bell's Pay It Forward program at our 2007 Christmas Party, and it's been going ever since.

When people interview for jobs at Bell Bank, or approach you for services, how often are they aware of the Pay It Forward program?

Pay It Forward is often part of what draws them to our company. People want to work at a company that embraces and empowers this kind of giving.

How do you manage the program logistically? Do you need a charitable gift receipt from every donation? Do employees need to report where their donations go? Do you trust employees to make their own decisions, and how do you prevent bad decisions?

> *Employees apply for their Pay It Forward funds, so the funds have to go through an approval process. The only restriction is that the funds don't go to an employee or an employee's family member. Employees are the true stewards of the program, and they work with human resources to access the funds for their chosen projects.*
>
> *We love the fact that other than that, employees are totally empowered to choose to help people in need or support causes they care about. Employees report on their projects through the application form, and we do ask that they document their gift with photos and video, whenever possible.*
>
> *We don't 1099 these funds, so they aren't taxed for our employees, and they don't have to donate only to 501(c)(3) organizations.*

Please share a favorite story about this program. How has it impacted you personally—or your team members, the recipients, the community?

> *There are so many great stories. You'll literally find dozens on our website at bellbanks.com/payitforward. One personal favorite would be "Smiles for Ryan," where employees at our Detroit Lakes, Minnesota, location pooled funds to support a little boy born with a condition that did not allow him to smile.*

He calls Bell "the smile bank" and has since had surgery and physical therapy that have him smiling.

How do you measure the success of this program outside of the monetary charitable giving?

The Pay It Forward program has truly changed all of our lives. It tangibly connects the work we do every day at the bank to how each of us makes a difference in the world around us. This kind of giving profoundly impacts us, the givers, as much as those who receive the donations. And it has opened our eyes and hearts to the needs around us, whether in our own community or across the world.

Moving to Action: Purpose
with Carol Grannis, Ed.D.

All you need is a journal, some uninterrupted time (30 minutes will do), and some vulnerability. Here are some exercises to get you moving forward in the area of purpose.

•

Carol Grannis, Ed.D., Chief Self Esteem Officer for SEB

5 Things You Can Do Right Now

1. Look at the current mission and vision statements (if you have them) for your company and/or your department.

2. Rewrite these statements off the top of your head based on what you think they should be.

3. Think about what product or service you sell, and write down the larger purpose that it embodies.

4. Survey your employees on what they view as your company's larger purpose.

5. Identify three local charitable organizations that provide a good fit with your larger company purpose.

Big Ideas in This Section

Your Life Manifesto. The pivotal idea around purpose is all about you. Successful leaders—heck, successful people—are very clear about their purpose in life. People who have a strong purpose (some refer to it as their "calling") have answered the question "What do I care about that's bigger than myself?" and aligned their actions with these beliefs. They put their time and money where their purpose is.

Give me a reason. The second big idea within this section is your ability to clarify and rally others around their purpose—in their own life and within your business.

<u>Business Purpose</u>: Your job is to make sure your staff

understands your organization's larger purpose. Even if you think your product is "bland," it's surely used in meaningful ways—in addition to providing good jobs for people to take care of themselves and their families. Keep in mind: Employees don't get inspired by a purpose to "make money for shareholders." They need a purpose that supports the success or care of others.

<u>Individual Purpose</u>: You have a unique opportunity to give your employees the space to answer the questions "What is my purpose in life?" and "What do I care about?" Knowing the answer to these questions can radically change the tenor of your relationships with your employees and the trajectory of their lives.

Journaling Exercises

"Your George Bailey Reason"

- Think about the big questions, like "What is my purpose?" and "Why am I here?" Then think about the character of George Bailey from *It's a Wonderful Life*.

Now answer these questions:

- What would have happened if I wasn't born?
- Who in my life have I had a profound impact on?
- Who is most likely to speak about me at my funeral, and what do I think they would say versus what would I want them to say?

- Which values in my life could use a little more attention? What impact would that attention have on me and others?

"Got a Strat Plan?"

- Think about how you rally others around a purpose.
- On a scale of 1–10, write down how clear you think your strategic plan is (1: You don't have one, but you know it's a good idea; 10: You have a clear strategy that you've shared with employees, and they could articulate it if asked.)

Now answer these questions:

- What's the impact of this number today?
- What impact would a clearer purpose have on your customers and employees?
- What could you do in the next week that would have a powerful impact on clarifying your purpose for your team?

Online Resources @ www.PeoplePurposeProfitsPlay.com

- Business Strategy Template
- Individual Scorecard for Employee with Work and Life Goals
- Creating a Service Manifesto for Yourself and Your Team

A Story to Tell: Jeff O'Mara

Jeff O'Mara receiving CPR after experiencing sudden cardiac arrest inside one of his Anytime Fitness gyms

In May 2010, my life changed forever, because it nearly ended. I owned two Anytime Fitness gyms at the time, and I was a regular exerciser—working out so often that I put the 20-year-olds to shame. Then on a normal, sunny day at my gym in North Vernon, Indiana—with no pain or discomfort as a warning—I froze up in the middle of a conversation and couldn't communicate. People told me later that I was making what sounded like a "cooing" sound, but actually it was just me trying to breathe. I wasn't having a heart attack. I was experiencing sudden cardiac arrest, which is worse. You usually die within minutes.

When one of the members called 911, the paramedics said to get me on the floor as safely as possible. When they did, my whole body contracted. At one point, I went completely lifeless, and that's when two of my personal trainers started performing CPR. One gave the breaths, the other did the compressions. Lucky for me, they had just gotten recertified to do CPR a month before. Minutes later, EMTs rushed in. They worked on me all the way to the hospital, but I didn't go to a local hospital. I was loaded onto a helicopter and flown to Indianapolis, 65 miles away. At the Indy hospital, I had to go on life support. In effect, I was dead. But somehow, I managed to come back to life. In fact, I'm proud to say that I was back on the elliptical machine a week later.

You might think that this is a story about the need to get in shape to avoid heart disease, but my case is slightly different. I have a perfectly strong heart, and the problem that day wasn't about clogged arteries, but electricity. I have a defibrillator now to shock me back to life should I ever have another episode, but the doctor told me that were it not for my voracious exercise regimen—not to mention those amazing trainers, EMTs, and doctors—I wouldn't have survived. Without becoming an Anytime Fitness member and then making the decision to put fitness at the center of my work life by buying into the company's greater mission, I wouldn't be alive today and telling you my story.

When something like this happens to you, you can't help but ask why. When I did that, I realized that I was spared for a reason, and I think it was to save someone else's life. So now I'm paying it forward any way I can. Anytime Fitness makes that easy, because when you buy into a business, you also join a family. Through that family, I'm saving lives every day by listening to my members, finding out what brought them into the club, and helping them reach their goals. I also tell them my story, and when they understand that fitness truly is a matter of life and death, they're more inspired than ever to get to a healthier place.

I now own 12 Anytime Fitness clubs in four states, with a 13th on the way. I'm forever grateful that I get to live out my purpose every day. Mostly, I'm happy simply for the gift of life, and I'm determined to help others live theirs to the fullest.

Jeff today

LOVE WORK

A Story to Tell: Mary Thoma & The Golden Girls

The Golden Girls (and Guys) of eastern Wisconsin

After years of caring for my ailing father, I was depressed and on the verge of diabetes. I had gained over 100 pounds, and I had gotten to the point where I looked happy on the outside but was dying on the inside. To make matters worse, the medications I was on cost $580 a month, which is almost $7,000 a year. None of this was sustainable, and I knew something had to change.

When my father passed, I decided it was time to take care of myself. I joined Anytime Fitness and worked with an amazing personal trainer to lose more than 100 pounds, but the story doesn't end there. I grew so tight with my new gym family that we started a little workout group. A least it started small. Eventually it grew to 27 members, and we started calling ourselves The Golden Girls.

Our main purpose was to get ourselves healthy, but we soon felt a bigger calling to help the community by holding fundraisers throughout the year. Probably our most memorable event was for "Bubba J." This little boy's heart was failing at 3 months old. He had a heart transplant at 9 months and his first heart attack at 2. Then cancer set in at 4. We decided we had to do something to help Bubba J and his family, so we organized a bratwurst fry at Anytime Fitness in Oshkosh.

Two weeks before the event, Bubba's uncle called me and asked who we were and why we were doing this. After I explained it to him, he said, "You guys are a godsend" at least four times in our 20-minute talk. When we met Bubba J's family, it just melted our hearts. His mom came up to me and said, "You must be Mary." Her eyes filled with tears, and she hugged me so hard I could barely breathe. I told her not to cry because we'd all be crying and we had brats to sell.

The whole event was awesome. People filled the streets, and it was heartwarming to see the community support. It was a day filled with joy and satisfaction, and even though Bubba J couldn't join us that day, we did eventually get to meet him. And his smile is worth everything to us.

To date, we've raised over $76,000 for people in need, and we expect to hit $100,000 in 2017. The local Chamber of Commerce has recognized our work, which is great, but that's not why we do it. We truly believe that The Golden Girls of Anytime Fitness will change the world. So we're just going to keep going.

The amazing Bubba J

A community service award given to The Golden Girls in 2016

— PART III —

Profits

> "Doing well is the result of doing good. That's what capitalism is all about."
>
> —Ralph Waldo Emerson

•

> "That's great, Ralph, but it's pretty damn hard to do good if you don't do well first."
>
> —Chuck & Dave

Formative Profit Moment

•

Back when I was a fitness club consultant in my 20s, I'd travel 10 months out of the year to various gyms to do marketing and membership blitzes. I got paid on commission based on the number of new memberships, so when a blitz went well, the checks would start rolling in.

When I was on the road, my parents would send me packets of mail from home, and I would send commission checks back for them to cash. After three weeks of commissions on a blitz that went well, I sent my parents a check for $5,700. When my mom called, I thought she was going to congratulate me on my success. Instead, she said, "Honey, are you selling drugs?"

—Chuck

One day, we got word that an Anytime Fitness franchisee couple was coming to our headquarters for a training session, so we invited them to lunch. They had recently been featured in one of our newsletters, and we wanted to congratulate them on something they'd done for one of their members: A single parent had been tragically killed in a car accident, leaving behind a daughter who was a senior in high school. The couple responded by holding a 5K walk/run fundraiser and rallying their staff and members to help pay for the daughter's college tuition. Their goal was to raise $5,000. In the end, they collected twice that.

We were eager to learn more about the success of this fundraiser, but we also never miss an opportunity to evaluate a franchisee's business. So before the lunch, we gathered their club's key performance indicators (KPIs), including number of members, base operating expenses, revenue from memberships, revenue from personal training, average pricing, and how well they were retaining members.

The first 20 minutes of the lunch was filled with warm fuzzies. We talked about the couple's amazing fundraising initiative and about how it fit with our strategy of getting local communities to see us as more than a gym. Then we turned our focus to their business performance.

We should mention that while "Minnesota Nice" is certainly in our genes, "Minnesota Passive-Aggressive" is not. We both have serious no-bullshit switches inside of us. When Dave flips that switch, he transforms back into the hard-nosed wrestler he was as a teenager. He asks blunt questions, and his eyes and body language say, "It's in your best interest to answer me honestly." Chuck is more of a sit-back-and-fold-his-arms kind of guy. He pulls a Jedi mind trick and somehow manages to become more detached and more engaged at the same time.

The couple's KPIs showed uneven profitability over the trailing 24 months, and we knew from experience that this financial rollercoaster was unhealthy and unsustainable. So our switches flipped, and between the four of us, the conversation went something like this:

So, let's talk about your business. How's it doing?

Oh, it's pretty good.

There's only two months left in the year. What are your revenue and profitability projections?

Awkward glance. No answer.

As a percent of revenue, how much will you do in personal training this year?

Um, we didn't bring those numbers today.

If we were to ask about your retention rate or average pricing, would you know those numbers right now?

I guess we weren't prepared for this talk . . .

That's fine, but how about this: Within a few pounds, do each of you know your current weight?

Confused nods.

When you drive, do you often check the gauge to see how much gas is left? And do you know the weather forecast back home for the next couple of days?

More nods.

If you're a business owner, isn't knowing the first set of numbers we asked for the equivalent of knowing your weight, the temperature outside, or how much gas is left in your tank?

We could sense they were taken aback by our questions, and maybe a little embarrassed. So we ended on a Minnesota Nice note, letting them know that while that didn't take anything away from their awesome fundraising efforts, they should see our talk as a learning opportunity: Entrepreneurs need to know their numbers, period. No exceptions.

Sometimes tough love can make people defensive, and we weren't sure how the couple would react once they returned home. Two months later, they sent us an email:

> "Thank you for the meeting two months ago. It had a big impact on both of us. Since then, we look over our numbers every week, and it's helping us run the business more effectively. We even set goals on improving them next year. Our current KPIs and KPI goals are attached. Thanks again; we are better because of it!"

That was the right response.

Up to this point, we've talked about the need to value and invest in people, as well as the importance of finding your organization's bigger purpose and infusing it into every aspect of your culture. Basically, the first two sections of this book have been the warm-and-fuzzy part of that lunch. Well, now it's time to flip the switch, because profits are the financial lifeblood of a sustainable company.

Like any large franchise, Anytime Fitness is a big company made up of thousands of smaller companies, so we've seen our share of business successes and failures over the last 20 years. We assume that you already have a product or service that someone's willing to pay for, so that's not what this section is about. This is about helping you turn a small profit into shit-loads of profits.[9]

In this P (Profits) section:

- We'll show you how to change your mindset when it comes to profits.

- We'll talk about how "lifestyle" is arguably your most valuable currency.

- We'll do a crash course in "Profits 101" and go over the nuts and bolts of financial measurement and success.

- We'll share a valuable outside perspective from the leader of a national brand that has merged profits and purpose in a highly contagious way.

---

[9] You probably won't find this term in an MBA textbook.

— CHAPTER 9 —

The Only P That Matters?

"Just win, baby!"

—Al Davis, Oakland Raiders owner, 1972–2011

The phone rings and jolts you out of a deep and comfortable slumber. It's Sunday. The clock says 5:08 a.m. And you already know why someone's calling. After a quick exchange with the caller, you leap out of bed, throw on shorts, a shirt, and a baseball cap and jump into your car. Eight minutes later, you're opening up your health club in front of a small group of angry members.

"This is the last time. I'm quitting!"

"This is bullshit!"

"We expect a refund this month!"

Inside, you run around frantically turning on lights, opening doors, and prepping the club for a busy day. When you go back to the front desk, an embarrassed employee slinks in and says she's sorry for oversleeping. You inform her that there's no need to apologize, because it's her last day.

•

When we co-owned three large stand-alone fitness clubs in our pre-Anytime Fitness days, we experienced this exact scenario far too often. The front-desk position at any big club is often a part-time job for high school and college kids, so early weekend shifts are like playing "responsibility roulette." To make matters worse, early-morning health club diehards are the last group you want to piss off (don't mess with anyone who's willing to work out at 5 a.m. on a Sunday morning—seriously). The turnover issue was costly and time-consuming, but the morning fire drill was even worse.

During this time, we were also learning a lot about other key areas of running a fitness business profitably. Our three clubs had been losing money before we took them over, and part of the challenge in making them profitable was turning wasted square footage into productive space. The gyms had all been built in the late '70s and early '80s, when racquetball courts, pools, whirlpools, and saunas were the hot thing. Our older members might have enjoyed these features, but we couldn't help but notice that our younger customers were far more focused on weight and cardio machines. So to make our space more useful, we filled the racquetball courts with treadmills, Stairmasters, exercise bikes, free weights, and resistance machines.

At the same time, we were also running complementary marketing and billing companies that helped round out our fitness club educations. The marketing business gave us an acumen for sales and direct-response marketing in the pre-internet and smartphone age, while the billing company (used to pay gym memberships) taught us even more about the numbers side of the business.

As we connected these dots, we started talking seriously about creating a new kind of "express sized" fitness center. By the summer of 2000, we felt close to pulling the trigger, but a key piece was still missing. We didn't know it yet, but that piece was directly related to those Sunday-morning club calls.

That fall, Chuck was driving southeast on Interstate 24, about an hour outside of Nashville. Near Tullahoma, Tennessee, a town of approximately 15,000 people, he visited one of the gyms that we were "blitzing" with marketing and membership efforts. Chuck was intrigued to see that the gym was small (less than 4,000 feet) and filled with only cardiovascular and weight equipment. Even more surprising was this: *Each member received a key to the gym.* We're talking the kind you unlock your home with, made at the local hardware store. Any member was free to access the gym anytime they wanted to, yet there were no cameras or security systems—just a sign near the door asking members to turn off the lights if they were the last to leave.

Chuck went back to the hotel to have a beer with our team, who had been working with this club for weeks, and he asked them if this small-town honor system was actually working. When they told him that members had no safety or service concerns about joining a club that was often unstaffed, he practically ran to the parking lot to make the most important phone call of his life.

"This is it! This is the missing piece to our express club model!"

We had always envisioned a franchise of smaller clubs containing only the most popular equipment, but we had assumed traditional operating hours and staffing requirements. By adding the "open 24/7" piece, we would empower members to work out on *their* schedules, not the club's. Giving members personal access allowed us to reduce payroll costs substantially—which meant we could eliminate the front-desk position, and thus those Sunday-morning phone calls and pissed-off members.

The days, weeks, and months after that seminal call are a blur. Every industry expert we talked to—including some big vendors in the fitness industry—told us that our concept wouldn't work because of member concerns over safety and service. But we charged ahead anyway. We didn't have experience running a franchise, but we were confident that we could open and operate one. We didn't have a ton of money, but we trusted that the capital investments of franchise owners could fuel our growth. And we knew that not every community's citizens were as trustworthy as Tullahomans, so we developed a software/hardware platform that could deliver the access and security we needed.

In May 2002, Eric Keller opened the first Anytime Fitness gym in Cambridge, Minnesota. Later that year, Jinell Abernethy opened club #2 in Duluth, and Tim Anderson opened #3 in Albert Lea. Fifteen years later: Jinell now owns five clubs in Duluth. Tim still operates his. And Eric now oversees our International Support division (and also has a good "Story to Tell" at the end of this section). The people who said our idea would never work? Many of them remain our most loyal vendors.

Our reason for sharing this anecdote isn't simply to tell one of the seminal moments in Anytime Fitness history; it's a "get real" moment for us and for you. Because as much as we've talked about people and purpose to this point, the truth is, our biggest concern in starting Anytime Fitness wasn't about either of those things (in fact, we were actively trying to minimize people to avoid unpredictability and get rid of those early-morning club openings). When we were developing our business model, we were concerned with profits, period. Because without profits, the other Ps simply can't exist.

Like Winning, Profits Are Contagious

In the course of working with Marc Conklin on writing this book, we got to talking about the state of affairs with his alma mater's football team. Notre Dame had just come off a miserable 4–8 season, and the alumni were screaming for a coaching change. Marc went off on how the next coach needed to address off-the-field issues, because the school prided itself on more than football. Just for fun, we posed a hypothetical question to him: If Notre Dame's next coach was a great guy, kept his players out of trouble, and brought the team's graduation rate to 100 percent, but the team never even came close to winning a national championship, would he be happy?

"Of course not!" he said.

And he's not alone. When's the last time you saw 60,000 people fill a stadium to cheer on their team's off-the-field conduct? Sure, fans love to see stories about their favorite athlete visiting a local hospital, but in sports, winning is the original performance-enhancing drug. It rewards teamwork, sacrifice, and hard work. Players are expected to work their butts off for it, and coaches are paid handsomely to make it happen.

We often compare a company org chart to a football team. On paper, every football team has similar positions: quarterback, wide receiver, tackle, etc. They all study each other's stats and game film, so what makes one team better than another? A mix of talent, execution, strategy, and adjustments. Same with a company org chart. Every company has similar positions: CEO, CFO, VPs in sales, marketing, IT, etc. So why do some companies win more versus others? The same mix of talent, culture, strategy, and adjustments.

Sometimes we'll show the following two images in meetings, and we'll tell our people to imagine their competitive counterpart on the other side of the line. Then we ask: Are you better than they are? Did we recruit a more talented individual? Do you have the right resources and the best game plan? As a team, do we have the right climate to problem-solve, make halftime adjustments, and collaborate better? Being just 1 percent better every day than the person across from you can add up to a huge difference over 200 workdays a year. And that's what profitability comes down to.

The Only P That Matters?

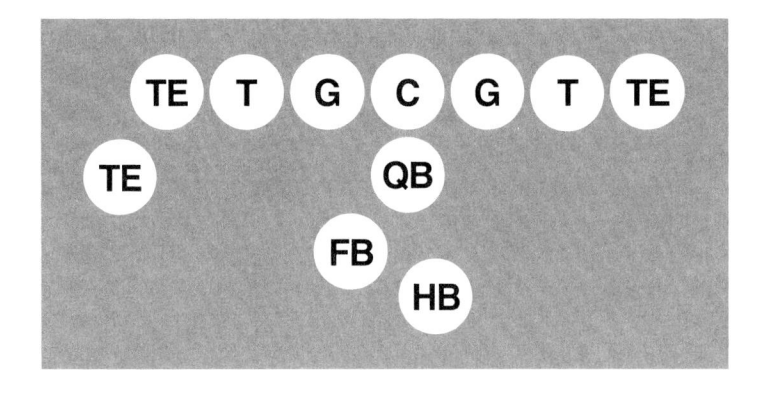

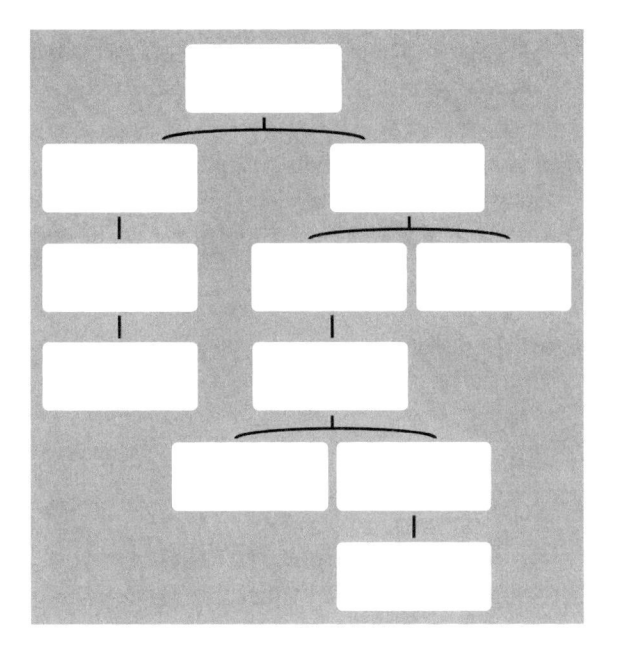

Think of your org chart like a football team: Each of your competitors has a counterpart on the other side. Are you better than they are at your position?

Like the New England Patriots, a profitable business can create its own gravity—drawing good people in and keeping them there. If your business doesn't make money, you can't attract and retain quality people, nor can you reinvest in them. When you're profitable, you're better able to spread the wealth—in recognition, professional growth opportunities, higher compensation, and an overall sense of accomplishment.

Although profits are the third P in this book (it sounds better that way), a strong case can be made for its actually being first in importance. After all:

- If you have a company with no sense of **purpose**, you're not leaving much of a legacy. But if you value **people**, have a strong sense of **play**, and deliver **profits**, you can still be successful to some degree.

- If your business doesn't truly value **people**, then it's hard to feel any real sense of pride in it. But if you still infuse a sense of **play** and **purpose** into it—and turn a **profit**—then you can survive for a while.

- An organization with no sense of **play** isn't a place we'd want to work, but you can still build a decent company that values **people**, has a sense of **purpose**, and earns **profits**.

- But you can't sustain a company on **people**, **purpose**, and **play** alone. Without **profits**, you spend all your time and resources on resuscitating your business. There's no room for purpose. There's no mood for play. And when people sense that a company is sinking, they jump ship.

Literally and figuratively, profits are your bottom line. If you want to expand or grow your business, your banker needs to see profitability. If you've taken on investors, they want to see the valuation of the business grow—and that's dictated by a steady climb in growth and profits. Most important, you as a leader need to see a return on your time, energy, and dedication to the business.

Invest to Grow

The real question on profits isn't *whether* you focus on them, but *how*. Is your approach to profitability healthy and sustainable, or obsessive and destructive? Does it enable and encourage the other Ps, or does it threaten to erode and undercut them?

We often see the relentless quest for short-term profits—especially at large, publicly traded companies. Businesses that fall into this trap will do anything and everything in their power to show a year-over-year quarterly profit gain on paper, and they're obsessed with boosting their stock price a couple of points to satisfy their most ardent investors. We certainly understand the pressures these businesses face. But we also know that this quick-fix approach can destroy an organization's culture—and, ironically, its profitability.

The profits litmus test for any business leader is "What do you do when your company's financial picture plateaus or hits a downturn?" These situations take you to a clear fork in the road: You can either retreat by reducing expenses to boost short-term profitability or invest in marketing, people, or products. If you define profitability purely as "top line" versus "bottom line," then your instinct is to cut costs, lay people off, reduce benefits, and move to single-ply toilet paper in all the bathrooms. That might make you feel better for five minutes, but what usually happens when you do that? People notice. Rumors spread. Employees start looking around and weighing their options. Morale quickly plummets. Profitability takes another hit. And now you're engaged in a race to the bottom.

The better alternative is to invest to grow. We learned this early in our entrepreneurial careers because, as a fitness club marketing company, we had to invest money every time we started a new promotion. Our value proposition to health club owners was simple: We'll invest our time and money into your marketing, and if we fail, you'll pay nothing. For every membership generated, we'd take a portion to pay for expenses and realize profits. Did we sometimes lose money with this approach? Yes, but no one in business gets a hit in every at bat. Over time, we certainly made more money than we lost, and the company lasted for nearly 15 years.

Our marketing experience conditioned us to invest for growth, and we used this strategy often during our three club takeovers prior to starting Anytime Fitness. In each situation, the previous club owners were faced with declining revenue and value in an aging facility saddled with stale equipment and programming. When we stepped in, we'd invest in new staff, new equipment, fresh programming, and interior and exterior upgrades. Some changes were cosmetic: We'd install new carpet and paint, and do a deep cleaning. Others were more significant: We'd convert racquetball courts into fitness rooms, or remove walls and raise ceiling heights to create more open spaces. Our initial takeover investments weren't cheap: between $200,000 and $400,000. But even today, we still embrace this investment mindset. And if someone on our team brings a well-crafted plan to invest in and grow the business, we'll almost always say yes.

Too often when a gym begins to struggle, the franchise owner gets a case of alligator arms with his or her checkbook. At a time when they need to invest, they look for ways to reduce expenses to maintain short-term profitability. Case in point: We once saw a franchise group open 14 Anytime Fitness gyms in Arizona in a short amount of time. Due to partnership turmoil, poor leadership, and irresponsible spending, they ended up on the brink of closing all of their clubs. Rather than let that happen, we deployed a turnaround team that stabilized all the clubs in a matter of weeks. We eventually resold them to new owners, kept them open, and returned them to profitability.

On the flip side, many of our individual franchisees have shown an impressive attitude of investment. Bobby Britton of Pearl, Mississippi, bought a struggling Anytime Fitness club and immediately invested his time and money into the business. He worked 12-hour days cleaning the club and getting to know every member. He put $50,000 into new equipment. And he put money into marketing, believing that it should be the third-largest spend every month after rent and payroll. In less than a year, Bobby more than doubled his membership and turned the club into a profitable, growing business. He won our annual Turnaround Club of the Year award, and he now owns a second Anytime Fitness.

Bobby Hines has a similar story. He took over a distressed club in Opelousas, Louisiana, and also made immediate investments into the business. The previous owner hadn't spent money to grow the club. Mirrors were broken. They had no personal training, had only a few part-time workers, and more members were leaving than joining. The first thing Bobby's team did was clean the club and make sure the equipment was working well. Then they hired personal trainers and started offering group classes and personalized support. Within a few months, Bobby doubled his membership and increased his personal training revenue.

Regardless of what business you're in, you have to invest to grow. As Warren Schatz, who co-owns 30-plus Anytime Fitness clubs, says, "When a business is running, most owners make the mistake of looking for ways to penny-pinch to increase margin. It's pretty simple: Money makes money." For you, that might be in a regular cadence of marketing. It might be a customer win-back program, a new piece of equipment, a software program. Or you might need to recruit highly paid, talented people to help you run and grow the business. It doesn't matter what you do: If you're in business, you should always be making investments to grow. Because in the end, you're either growing or dying.

Our Profit Epiphany

Prior to starting a franchising business, we held a fairly traditional view of leadership: The reason you hire people is to grow your company's profits, period. So when it came to our employees, we'd show up to work every day with a "what have you done for the business?" mindset. Frankly, we didn't think twice about this mentality until we entered the world of franchising and were confronted with an unavoidable truth: Our success was now 100 percent tied to the successes of each of our franchise owners.

This new reality required us to flip our perspective. We realized that our franchisees didn't work for us; we worked for them. So "helping our franchisees succeed" became our primary mission. To support that, we invested our time and money into tools, training, and ongoing education to help them grow their businesses. And that allowed us to grow and maintain our profits.

This mindset applies to any business or industry—not just franchising—and it needs to happen in a pay-it-forward way across all levels of leadership. For example, while we focus on helping our Anytime Fitness gym owners succeed, they need to focus on helping their personal trainers build a book of business. Similarly, while we look for ways to help our Waxing the City franchise owners build their business, they need to help their body-waxing technicians increase their expertise, product sales, and client base. No matter what business you're in, everyone within it is an "intrapreneur," and their individual success will always funnel to your bottom-line profitability.

Whether you employ salespeople, bartenders, waitresses, hair stylists, or anyone who directly sells your company's product or service, it's your job to help each employee excel at their job through ongoing training, the right tools, a good team, and a clear direction. But most of all, people need a leader who cares about their success and is eager to invest in it. Remember: A leader builds people, and people build profits. So to paraphrase John F. Kennedy, "Ask not what your employees can do for you, but what you can do for your employees."

That is, until it's clear that things just aren't going to work out. Then it's a different story.

Tough Love & The Loyalty Trap

Imagine this scenario: One of your longest-standing employees has just walked into your office and taken a seat across your desk. As you look at him, you think about how he's been with you since those scrappy start-up days. He was there when everybody answered the phone, made sales, and solved IT problems. He was there when you had your first crappy offices that smelled like mold and cat litter. You knew him when he found a partner and started a family. You sent flowers to the church when his mother died. And when he leans in and rests his arms on your desk, you can't help but notice the big tattoo of your company logo bulging from his forearm.

"You wanted to see me?" he says.

"Yes. We've taken a long look at things, and this has been a very difficult and painful decision, but we've decided to remove you from your role."

These are the moments that truly test leaders, because when people and loyalty butt heads with profits and competence, the latter must win. The key to survival is avoiding what we call "the loyalty trap," and we've found that this is one of the hardest and most important elements of creating and maintaining a high-performance culture. To be sure, we see terminations as the last resort, not the first. And we never let an employee go until we've looked inward and asked ourselves if we did a good enough job onboarding, training and supporting them.

But sometimes tough love is necessary—not only in letting an employee go, but also in guarding against complacency, which can be a gateway drug to undertime. Entitlement is something you need to nip in the bud, and even the best teams need an occasional trip to the cultural chiropractor. To best capture how we've handled that rare situation, we'll share an actual email that Chuck sent on Aug. 9, 2016, just a few months after we moved into our current headquarters building. To provide some context, we had been answering questions from our "Just Ask" box (mentioned in Chapter 4, "Designing a People Culture"), and we noticed that we were getting more and more frivolous requests for personal or luxury items at the new office, rather than work-related questions about how to positively impact our members and franchise owners. Our fears about moving into a new building seemed to be coming true, as some of our new employees—those who hadn't worked in the scrappier, more modest office environments of years past—were sounding a bit spoiled.

Best Team in Franchising,

It's Friday afternoon, and I'm halfway to the cabin, stopping for supplies and to check email, and I read some first-world-problem "Just Ask" questions about things like coffee and solicitors. During the remainder of my drive, my mind races: Who is asking these questions? Who actually thinks this way?

Franchisees are investing their life savings with us and putting their faith in us, and people are asking about better-tasting coffee? Given the challenges and required changes ahead, this is what our team is troubled with? Instead of bringing out our best, is this amazing building bringing out the worst in some of us? Are we losing our edge? Our hunger? Our consuming passion to serve franchisees and members?

Not wanting to believe that our employees are becoming this entitled, I briefly consider that these questions must have been written as a joke to see how Dave and I respond, but considering past questions about blow dryers, grills, and unclean kitchens, it's clear that some of our peers have become polluted with complacency and workplace privilege.

It's unfathomable that any of these questions came from team members that worked back in our first office in West St. Paul, or spent any meaningful time in Hastings, St. Paul, or Denver. They know our values of hard work, humility, an unrelenting thirst to improve, and a deep appreciation for the difficulty of our climb.

Despite all the awards, they still embody "earned not given." Therefore, these questions must be coming from some of our recent team members who may be unaware of our indefatigable and scrappy DNA.

Whoever it is, let me be very clear: If you don't like the coffee, don't drink it. And if you don't know how to handle a solicitor, you are not smart enough to work here. If you have the luxury to whine about this shit, you're not working hard enough.

Look, the bar is being raised. The burden of our accountability to every stakeholder is getting heavier. Our franchisees invested in us. They deserve our very best, and every department should feel the pressure to deliver results and value.

The climb ahead is steeper and more difficult than the climb to get us here. If you don't have the grit, mindset, or perseverance to keep climbing, get off the f&$king mountain! I'm serious. If you don't have what it takes to keep climbing, spend the weekend updating your résumé, surfing LinkedIn, and quietly planning a graceful way to exit. Maybe you want to work at a coffee shop. I hear they have great-tasting coffee. If you don't, and only pretend that you bleed purpose, then our culture will find you and push you out.

Earned not given until I'm 6 feet under,
—Chuck

How can we talk like this after spending dozens of pages championing our "people" cred? Because "people" is bigger than any individual person. Despite our never-ending quest to achieve the most people-friendly business on the planet, we've often said things to our employees like "we love you, but we will fire you," "our brand is bigger than any one person," and "everyone is expendable." The reason is simple: Our mantra of fitness, life, and employment is "Earned Not Given," and it's important that no one, including us, take their tenure for granted.

Maybe that's why this email was strongly supported by the vast majority of our people—especially longtime team members and A players. Soon after we sent it, we noticed general intensity and nonverbal communication crank up a few notches. It gave permission for other leaders to hold their people accountable, and peer-to-peer accountability surged as well. We didn't change the basic rules on "Just Ask" feedback, yet we also noticed that the questions we received became more relevant.

Remember that high-performance quadrant we referenced in Chapter 4, "Designing a People Culture"? Sometimes focusing on that quadrant means you have to let people go who simply can't maintain their position. It's hard to lose loyal, hardworking employees—especially when they're essentially *good but not good enough.* In our 15-plus years of business, we've had to fire people with Anytime Fitness tattoos who fit well into the company culturally, but whose expertise and ability to achieve results couldn't keep up with the business. It's a gut-wrenching decision, because you're essentially telling someone that while you love their heart, their brain isn't measuring up.

This situation is especially prominent in successful start-ups. Entrepreneurs often begin their businesses by hiring family, friends, and associates who can wear dozens of hats. The struggle for survival forges strong bonds. And when the business grows, these entrepreneurs give new positions to these pioneer employees as a reward for their hard work and loyalty. As we've learned, this doesn't always work out. And when it doesn't, you're faced with a decision that will define the future of your business, your culture, and your leadership effectiveness: Will you keep the pioneer employee or replace them with someone better?

If you keep them, then that area of the business will never reach its full potential. The rest of the team will notice. It'll send the message that you care more about protecting one person than serving the best interests of the entire organization. And it'll send the message that you value friendship over performance—injecting poison politics into the culture. The right decision is obvious; it just isn't easy.

Over the years, some of our most difficult days have been ones where we had to terminate loyal team members who were instrumental in our earlier success. These are people who worked countless hours on behalf of the business, and who possessed great character, work ethic, and motivations. But as the team grew and roles became more complex, they came to lack the technical, strategic, or leadership ability to adapt and perform. Sometimes the temptation is to reassign these people to lower positions. But the most common result of that is a person who feels wronged or embarrassed by accepting a demotion—and whose disappointment becomes toxic to others.

The more you grow, the higher the stakes get, and the more you have to treat individual people with what we call "detached love." Every one of our stakeholders is important individually. But ultimately, our profits come from attracting, engaging, supporting, and retaining health club members and franchise owners. Our business, like any other, is a merciless arena filled with an army of competitors. Therefore, we need the most talented people in the right positions to navigate the company to success.

In sports, winning trumps the player. With great bands, it's about the music, not the musician. As a leader, you must always put the organization as a whole above any individual employee.

But you must also define "profits" in a broader, less traditional way . . .

— CHAPTER 10 —

The Currency of Lifestyle

"Great Businessperson, Lousy Parent"

—The honest tombstone of most entrepreneurs

A bout four years into Anytime Fitness, a successful franchisee approached us for advice. He'd opened three profitable gyms and was trying to figure out whether to make a sizable investment in the strip mall where one of them was located. This would diversify his portfolio of assets and open up new revenue streams from other businesses, but it would also require a large capital investment, increase his total debt, and make it harder for him to open more gyms.

"What would you do?" he asked. "Open more clubs or buy the entire strip mall?"

He expected a simple answer, but he didn't get one. We knew how his clubs were performing, but we also knew a few key items about his personal life—like the fact that he had a second child on the way and that his wife wanted to quit her job to help him run the business.

Our conversation went something like this:

So how many more kids do you plan on having?

Three or four; we're not sure. Why do you ask?

Well, with a larger family, you'll probably want a bigger house with new furniture, right? You might want a pool, a big yard, a fence, a riding lawn mower. You'll probably need an SUV. If your wife helps at the club, you'll need day care and preschool in the early years. Have you considered private or public schooling beyond that?

Um . . .

Do you have a comfortable rainy-day fund? Have you started saving for retirement? If your wife leaves her job, have you priced out health insurance?

Not yet . . .

You'll probably want to take your kids to Disney World and to see the grandparents a couple of times a year. Should we go on?

•

The fact is, if you're a business leader, your life is going to change over time, and you need to design your business to support your life. This is a common mistake entrepreneurs make, because they often don't think broadly enough or far enough beyond the creation stage. But before you get strategic about your business, you need to get strategic about your life. In other words, your business should support your lifestyle, not the other way around. After our conversation, our friend decided to reassess his situation. He passed on the real estate deal to conserve his capital and build a rainy-day fund. He eventually opened a fourth club, but it was near his other clubs, so it didn't impede his lifestyle. A few years later, he sold his four clubs. And last we heard, he was coaching his kids in three sports. Well done!

The point is this: When we talk about profits within the 4 Ps, we mean more than money. Today more than ever: *Lifestyle is currency, and achieving balance is both the ultimate goal and the hardest challenge.*

Hey, we get it. We know what it's like to be completely consumed by your business. We don't know anyone within our circle of friends, family, or acquaintances who's worked longer or harder than we have over the last 15 years. We've sacrificed plenty, and we'd rather not calculate the countless hours that we've spent on airplanes, on phone calls, answering emails, or just thinking about the business day and night. We're deeply grateful to our spouses for this, because being married to an entrepreneur probably deserves its own support group. We spend a lot of time on business-related travel, but even when we're home, we're often physically present and mentally absent (or so we've been told). Our minds are often busy solving problems, scheming new ideas, or thinking of new ways to improve the business—and most of you probably know exactly what we're talking about.

But as we reflect on the growth of Anytime Fitness, one of our proudest achievements is the fact that we've never had to sacrifice raising our families. Too often, we've read about the maniacal entrepreneur who ignores his spouse and children and ends up regretting it years later. We may not have made every game or school event, but our batting averages have been pretty good overall. And along the way, we've found time to coach, volunteer, and spend hours shooting hoops, playing soccer, swimming, and pulling our kids behind the boat.[10]

Our love for work is still overshadowed by our love for our families, and we've always been intentional about working to live versus living to work. Many of our franchisees feel the same way, and it's gratifying to see how many of them have improved their personal health and lifestyles by opening one or more of our clubs. Here are just three of many examples:

---

[10] For our international readers, I should point out that in Minnesota, this term refers to waterskiing.

Andy Gundlach (Madison, Wisconsin)

When he was an operations director for a national fast-food chain, Andy lived an unhealthy, stressed-out existence. Although he was good at what he did and learned a lot on the job, he lacked passion. When he made the shift to becoming an entrepreneur and opened his first Anytime Fitness club in 2006, his attitude and lifestyle completely transformed.

Andy now owns 30 gyms in southern Wisconsin and takes in about $18 million in annual revenue. He wouldn't complain about the money, but what he values even more is the fact that he's now filled with energy. He's eager to get up in the morning and work out in one of his clubs, and he's stronger and healthier than ever before (seriously, look at him: he'll kick your ass). He thrives on talking to members about their fitness goals and helping them get there. And because he has built his own corporate infrastructure, he actually takes more vacations than ever before.

Paige Peterson (Oakland, Nebraska)

Paige describes her pre-Anytime life as "a boring CPA lifestyle in which I would shut the door, do my bookwork, and hope that nobody would bother me." Tired of the isolation, Paige took a big step forward when she opened an Anytime Fitness gym in Oakland (Nebraska, that is). As soon as she did, everything changed.

Like Andy, Paige has improved her own health by working out in her gyms early in the morning (she now owns six), and this helps her train as a marathon runner. She loves having the flexibility to be home every morning to make breakfast for her kids. But most dramatically, she's discovered her inner extrovert. Now her door is always open. She loves being out on the floor with her members, and her bigger purpose in life is to bring greater fitness to her small community.

Tony Black (Indianapolis, Indiana)

Tony used to live a monotonous corporate lifestyle that's probably familiar to many people reading this book. In addition to working long hours, he spent so much time at conferences around the country that he started collecting the plastic lanyards. It was a lifestyle that paid the bills but added little value beyond that.

Tony took a risk by leaving his white-collar world and opening an Anytime Fitness gym in Indianapolis, and his personal transformation has been impressive. Today, he's not only happier in his work life but also recognizes that he's a more patient and positive person overall. For the first time, he actually enjoys going to his job, because he no longer thinks of it as work. He's there for his two kids in a way that he never was before. He loves the chance to interact with members and help them get healthier. And he takes great pride in the fact that nearly every day, someone comes up to him and says simply "thank you."

Andy, Paige, and Tony are shining examples of how we should all define profits in our business and personal lives: Loving what you do. Not needing to hit the snooze button. Going to that basketball game, band concert, or school play. These things ultimately carry far more value than money.

As a leader, you need to love what you do. When you achieve that, then you can create a culture that makes your stakeholders profit as well.

But of course, you also need to know the basics.

— CHAPTER 11 —

Profits 101

"Things are always going to go wrong. People make mistakes. I know I do. It's how you resolve it that matters most. Listen, be open to criticism, resolve it with speed and empathy, and take responsibility."

—Marcus Lemonis from TV's *The Profit*

Now that we've talked big picture and defined profits in a broader way, let's get down to the nitty gritty. While this material might be a remedial course for some of you, in our experience, leaders of small to midsize businesses are often afraid to admit what they don't know. (Heck, we didn't start off knowing any of this; we had to figure it out for ourselves.)

In a nutshell, here are the basic "what to knows" for running a profitable business.

Know Your Numbers

After 15 years of working with small and midsize business owners, the most common mistake we see them make is not knowing their financials and key performance indicators (KPIs). If you can play fantasy football and track stats on dozens of players, then you possess the skills to measure your profitability. The most important numbers include these:

- **Income Statement:** This is a report of your company's financial performance over a specific accounting period. You assess your financial performance by giving a summary of how the business incurs its revenues and expenses through both operating and nonoperating activities.

- **Balance Sheet:** This is a statement that summarizes your assets, liabilities, and shareholders' equity at a specific point in time. These three balance-sheet segments give investors an idea of what your company owns and owes, as well as the amount invested by shareholders.

- **Cash Flow:** This is a financial snapshot computed by subtracting your operating expenses from the money your company generates during normal business activities. When your operating cash inflow exceeds your cash outflow, then congratulations! You're operating in the black.

- **Gross Margin:** If you're a small-business owner, you should know exactly how much it'll cost you to purchase your goods, as well as how much you'll need to sell those goods or services to turn a profit. Gross margin reflects how much money you have left after the actual cost of your merchandise is subtracted from the selling price. If this figure is low and not sufficient to cover your operating costs—such as salaries, rent, marketing, and utilities—then you're likely not charging enough for your products and services.

- **Net Income:** This one is closely related to cash flow, and it's what you get when you subtract all your expenses, including taxes, from your income. It's not adjusted for items like depreciation. Like cash flow, your net profit is a good indicator of whether you're making or losing money.

- **EBITDA (Earnings Before Interest, Taxes, Depreciation, and Amortization):** EBITDA is essentially your net income with interest, taxes, depreciation, and amortization (paying off a debt on a fixed schedule) added back to it. Because it eliminates the effects of financing and accounting decisions, you can use it to compare "apples to apples" when it comes to profitability levels between companies and industries.

- **Assets, Liabilities, and Revenue:** We could explain these basic terms, but if you don't already know them, then you should seriously consider selling your business. ;)

Know Your Customers

When it comes to customer data, small and midsize businesses have a tremendous advantage today versus just 10 years ago. In the past, only large companies had the capital and resources to make deep data dives. But with the rise of digitization, software as a service (SaaS) offerings, and affordable cloud computing, companies of all sizes can obtain insightful consumer insights and data.

With these tools now readily available, there's simply no excuse not to know these areas:

- **Demographics:** At a minimum, know your customers' age, income, gender, ethnicity, and education level.

- **Lifetime Value:** Track the amount of money a customer spends with you over the entire relationship with your business.

- **Buying Habits:** Document frequency of purchase, average spend per purchase, and most common items purchased.

- **Customer Satisfaction:** Take advantage of today's excellent tools (especially social media and Net Promoter Score[11]) to measure ongoing customer satisfaction, along with reasons why they bought (or stopped buying) your product or service. Even better, engage with them!

Know Your Industry & Competitors

No matter what industry you're in, we're guessing that it's changing fast. When we look back at the last 40 years, it's crazy to think of all the trends in fitness that have come and gone. We've seen the consumer spotlight move all over the place—toward racquet sports, weight lifting, aerobics, Stairmasters, Nautilus machines, Pilates, Spinning, group exercise, women-only clubs, big-box discount clubs, and, most recently, boutique studios, heart-rate training, and wearable activity trackers.

It's your job to anticipate these trends, and—more importantly—to decide if and how to react to them. Reactiveness is an underrated skill in business leaders today. We romanticize the idea of visionary, future-focused leadership, but our last 15 years have been mostly about adapting to new situations. The truth is, the nimble team that *responds* will win the profits game every time. After all, top-level coaches don't just make a game plan; they also make halftime adjustments. And if you're slow to react, then you might just go the way of Blockbuster or the PalmPilot.

At Anytime Fitness, we've made plenty of strategic calls. You can't expect to get them all right, but we have a pretty good track record. We decided not to engage in the price war spurred by the big-box discount clubs, and we've embraced technology—especially as an enabler for better health and accountability outside the gym environment. We've also recognized some things that will never change, like the fact that most people don't see results in fitness unless they feel welcomed, challenged, and supported by other human beings.

We encourage you to measure your organization against industry benchmarks. With the abundance of data available, businesses of all sizes can obtain comparable metrics and use them to make good decisions.

Know Your Strategy

In our experience working with businesses over the last 20 years (Anytime Fitness and beyond), we've found that most owners and leaders don't create a strategic plan. If they do, they either follow it in a sloppy way or ignore it altogether. That isn't a criticism; it's actually a confession. Because for the first 15 years running our small businesses, we definitely fell into the "sloppy execution" category.

A solid strategic plan is like a roadmap for your business. It's supposed to help you navigate in the short and long terms, and it should be designed to save you time and resources. Particularly for entrepreneurs, a strategic plan is a buffer against the temptation to chase every new idea (another tendency we've been guilty of over the years).

You can approach strategy from lots of different angles, but our preferred method for effective planning is the following:

Develop a Strategy Team

Based on your company's size, bring people together who represent the various functions of your business. You'll need front-line people who personally interact with the customers, but you should also include a savvy outsider—such as your banker, your accountant, or another successful business person. Once you get everyone in the room, create a no-title culture. Everyone should feel equal to weigh in on the business, offer ideas, provide constructive feedback, and ask pointed questions.

Do a SWOT Analysis

If you're not familiar with "SWOT," it stands for Strengths, Weaknesses, Opportunities, and Threats. Looking at those four elements as they apply to your business gives you a great framework to assess and improve your entire organization:

Strengths: What separates you from the competition? What do you do better than anybody else? What are your advantages when it comes to finances, organizational structure, products, and culture—or for that matter: people, purpose, profits, and play?

Weaknesses: What are the areas where you know you're vulnerable? Where does the competition kick your butt? The key here is to be honest. No one likes to admit their weaknesses, but you can't improve if you don't acknowledge them.

Opportunities: When looking at your strengths, what tangible opportunities do they present? Are you better able to create superior products? Get them to market faster? Do you have a window to lure a competitor's talent or win the loyalty of their customers?

Threats: *What internal and external factors could potentially harm your business? Are there issues with company culture or attracting talent? Is your industry facing cheaper competition overseas or online? Is the economy approaching a recession that might affect demand?*

If you're doing a SWOT analysis with a small group, one useful method is to put these four quadrants on a wall with space under each letter. Give each person in the room a stack of Post-it Notes, and ask them to write down what they see as the Strengths, Weaknesses, Opportunities, and Threats to the business. In addition to delivering the best analysis, this kind of exercise will empower and energize your team.

Prioritize the SWOT

Once your SWOT is complete, the team should look over the collection of Post-its and identify common answers, and then discuss where to prioritize the company's resources to take advantage of your biggest opportunities, protect against your biggest threats, maximize your biggest strengths, and overcome your biggest weaknesses.

Weigh each idea or initiative for greatest economic impact on the business. In doing so, consider the economic gain minus the capital expenditures or other company resources you'd need to achieve the goal. The group must be aware of the realistic capabilities and resources to carry out the strategic plan. And try to limit your strategies to two or three big goals for the year. It's easy to fall into the trap of wanting to do everything, but you'll want to keep your team focused on the initiatives that will drive the greatest economic gain to the business. Also make sure that your strategy drives your annual budget. Many business leaders—especially at small to midsize companies—make the mistake of signing onto budgets without allowing for the financial support that will accomplish their strategic goals.

Write It Down, Measure, and Meet

Once you've decided on your best few initiatives, write out your strategic plan. Include the tactics and resources necessary to accomplish each objective, as well as the timelines needed to complete them. Based on the size of your team, appoint someone to "own" each initiative, and measure your progress frequently along the way.

How often should you meet—and for how long? This is a common question we get from business owners, and we don't have a perfect answer. As our business has grown over the years, we've adjusted the rhythm of our meetings. And frankly, we've rarely felt like we've found the perfect cadence (even when we have, we've quickly had to change it to adapt to growth). As a rule of thumb, we recommend meeting for 60–90 minutes every other week, with a more substantial three- to four-hour meeting once a quarter. But the frequency of your meetings will actually depend on the trust, experience, performance, and competence of the individuals or teams—and the importance or complexity of the initiative. If one of our teams continues to demonstrate consistent performance, we may cut meetings back to every other week or once a month. As other teams ramp up and add new employees, we might meet with them once a week.

Keep in mind, though, that a productive meeting is measured by impact, not time. To give your meetings the greatest impact:

- Circulate an agenda and make sure everyone takes the time to prepare. Set aside time to identify problems, but get your team in the habit of thinking about *solutions* as well.

- Make sure you hear everyone's perspective. (Remember: When people weigh in, they buy in.)

- Don't attempt to "boil the ocean" in every meeting. Stay focused on improving one to three things.

- Insist that people take notes, and keep an ongoing journal to map the team's progress. If someone can't make it, share the notes with them.

"Playing with House Money"

Ever since we sold a minority percentage of our business to a private equity firm, we've heard dozens of business and investment community leaders say, "Congratulations! Now you're playing with house money!" If you're not familiar with this phrase, "playing with house money" is a casino expression for a player who has won back and pocketed the money they walked in with, and is now betting only with their winnings (the casino's money). Because this isn't technically their money, gamblers make riskier wagers in this situation—and, of course, they usually lose.

We know that people's intentions are good when they say this, but here's the truth: Despite the fact that we're never going to have to worry about our personal finances, we feel more financial pressure than ever before. Why? Because to us, playing with house money points to a different truth: We're always playing with the actual house money of people who count on us.

As a leader, you play a major role in the finances of your employees, investors, and, in our case, franchise owners. No matter what size or kind of business you run, your employees rely on a stable income to pay their mortgage and raise a family. In addition to that, we know that when someone signs a franchise agreement with us, they're entrusting us with a significant portion of their life savings. In some cases, they're even taking loans from family members.

For this and other reasons, we find any casino analogy to be flawed from the start. Your business isn't a game with winners and losers. You win as a team, and you each have a stake in each other's success. As a leader, you should never take these responsibilities lightly. Unlike a gambler, you must be bold without being reckless, and you must balance your actions to both grow and protect your stakeholders' money.

Along these lines, some people wonder why we've "stuck around" (read: not cashed out) at Anytime Fitness. This same question is asked of many successful entrepreneurs. Once you've exceeded your personal financial dreams, why keep working your ass off and losing sleep over money? For us, the answer is simple: It was never about the money to begin with;

it was about the idea, the vision, the people, and the challenge to grow a meaningful business. If "playing with house money" changes you as a leader—if you find that it truly is about the Benjamins—then it's probably time to get out.

Money helps us keep score, but it's not something to play with—especially if it's never really yours. Knowing your role as a leader starts with understanding what's at stake. Remember, "profit" has two meanings: As a noun, it refers to financial gain. But as a verb, "to profit" simply means to gain an advantage or benefit.

Being a leader means understanding your role in both—like our next interviewee.

---

[11] NPS is an index that measures the willingness of customers to recommend your products or services to others. Google it!

— CHAPTER 12 —

An Outside Perspective: Suzanne DiBianca

"The business of business is to improve the state of the world."

Suzanne DiBianca, EVP, Corporate Relations and chief philanthropy officer of Salesforce

Few people understand the relationship between profits and purpose better than Suzanne DiBianca of Salesforce. Since the well-known software company sparked a worldwide revolution with its "Pledge 1%" campaign, more than 2,000 companies have agreed to give 1 percent of their product, equity, and time to improve communities around the world. We asked Suzanne to tell us more about the Pledge 1% program, and to offer her perspective on how even small to midsize companies can use their profits to fuel their purpose.

Pledge 1% is a fantastic idea. How did it come about?

> Salesforce's corporate philanthropy model has been baked into our ideals since the company was founded 17 years ago. Our concept was simple: Leverage Salesforce's technology, people, and resources to improve communities throughout the world. We called our integrated philanthropic approach the 1–1–1 model, and since its introduction, we've given more than $160 million in grants, worked 2 million volunteer hours in communities around the world, and provided more than 31,000 nonprofits and educational institutions with the use of our technology.
>
> With this great success, we were compelled to share the idea with other like-minded institutions. That's why we introduced Pledge 1% in 2014. One of the most exciting moments for us was when Atlassian, a Pledge 1% company, went public in December 2015. Atlassian was one of the first companies to join the Pledge 1% movement, and their successful IPO demonstrated that the model works and can have a meaningful impact.

Economist Milton Friedman once said, "The social responsibility of a business is to increase profits." Why does Salesforce believe in serving a purpose beyond profits? Is it idealism, pragmatism, or a little bit of both?

With all due respect, we disagree with Friedman on this point. It's been disproven many times. According to Wharton,[12] companies with high worker satisfaction generally produce alphas, or above-average stock returns, compared to their peers. At Salesforce, we believe that the business of business is to improve the state of the world, and if you build a great company, you attract great talent and retain employees who want to create purposeful work.

To a business leader at a smaller organization, or a start-up with a negative burn rate, Pledge 1% may appear too daunting—or they might think they're too small to make a difference. What would you tell that start-up or a small-business owner doing less than $300K in annual revenue?

I would tell them that they can start at any time, but to start small. Pledging 1% doesn't have to be about money. It can also be about time, about volunteerism. Is there a nearby school where your employees could donate their time to staff a field trip? Pledge 1% is just as much about the people and product as it is about monetary contribution. Salesforce had 50 employees when we started the early versions of what would later become the 1–1–1 model. It's never too early to take a pledge. Bottom line: There are always ways to get involved, and by doing so, you'll inspire your employees and attract the right kind of talent.

How do you weave or operationalize the Pledge 1% into your workplace culture?

Incorporating Pledge 1% into a workplace culture doesn't have to be difficult. The most important thing is to give the pledge a name and an owner who's responsible for it. Commit to one project for the year and get extremely involved. For example, if you decide to make volunteerism at a school your project, learn the students' names. The companies that are most successful are the ones who make Pledge 1% part of their brand and culture.

Does the element of purpose help a company attract and retain talented people, and thus improve their profitability?

Today's top talent wants to work at a company with a meaningful mission and purpose. This is a premise that we have seen borne out here at Salesforce. Our workforce is engaged and proud to be part of a company that prioritizes doing good in the world. There's no silver bullet for measuring that, of course, but we see it play out in volunteerism. Employees who participate in our volunteer efforts tend to excel down the road. It's an early indicator of leadership and activism.

Moving to Action: Profits
with Carol Grannis, Ed.D.

All you need is a journal, some uninterrupted time (30 minutes will do), and some vulnerability. Here are some exercises to get you moving forward in the area of purpose.

•

Carol Grannis, Ed.D., Chief Self Esteem Officer for SEB

5 Things You Can Do Right Now

1. Write down all the ways you've invested in your business over the last year. For every investment, think about the *return* or value of that investment. If you haven't had many investments, what investment could you make within the next 12 months that would have the biggest impact?

2. Write down the names of your longest-tenured employees. Are they still with your business because of their performance and value, or is it possible that you're holding onto them because of a sense of loyalty?

3. Write down what you value in your life. Does your current business support your ability to live out these values? If yes, congratulations. If not, write down three things you could do.

4. Complete a SWOT analysis as described in this section. Share it with your team members and ask them to weigh in and add to it.

5. Look at how you're using your business profits in a larger context. As Suzanne DiBianca suggested, write down a focus your business could use (like Pledge 1%) to give back, support, or share with those in need.

Big Ideas in This Section

Mind your own business.
The first focus of the profits section is about understanding all facets of your business. How do you keep score? How do you

know when you're winning? Losing? What are the data points that tell you when you need to change tactics? KPIs are a great place to start. Create your own scoreboard that tells you what you need to know to lead your business, and then review it on a regular basis.

When the going gets tough, invest.
To grow your business, you must invest in it. It's normal to look for ways to cut costs when your business doesn't perform, but this is a short-term gain. Profits require steadfast commitment and a focus on long-term strategies that will get you back to a positive cash flow.

It's not just about the money.
Easy to say when you have money, but this concept is powerful. It's about designing your business to support your life, and to do that, you have to answer the question "What kind of life do I want?" This is about the currency of your lifestyle and working to live, not living to work.

Homework, homework, homework.
You don't have to go to business school to run a successful business, but you do have to study your trade and know your industry. Successful business owners are curious about their business and constantly seek ways to meet their customers' ever-changing needs. Stay ahead of the pack by being diligent about your strategic plans and assessing your business' strengths, weaknesses, opportunities, and threats. These are your keys to innovation and survival.

Journaling Exercises

"Your Shark Tank Moment"

- Pretend that you're going in front of Mark Cuban on the TV show *Shark Tank*. Are you prepared for the questions he'll ask you?

Now answer these questions:

- Do I know my sales, costs, valuation, gross margin, and net income off the top of my head?
- What value do I bring to the business personally?

"VIP KPIs"

- On a scale of 1–10 (1: Nonexistent; 10: Mastery), rate your focus on your KPIs.

Now answer these questions:

- If my number is 10, who else in our business could/should know our KPIs?
- What impact would this have on our business?
- If my number is less than 10, what can I do to move this number up?
- What would happen if I did nothing to improve it?

Online Resources @ www.PeoplePurposeProfitsPlay.com

- Business Strategy Template
- SWOT Analysis Template
- Life Value Checklist

A Story to Tell: Eric Keller

Pioneer Anytime Fitness club owner Eric Keller

I worked for Chuck and Dave at Southview Athletic Club, and I can still remember the night in January 2002 when I overheard Dave talking about their plans to start a new chain called "All the Time Fitness" or something like that. As I was running a mop and bucket behind an electric buffer, I thought to myself, "What the hell am I doing here?" Little did I know how much I would profit from that question, in many ways.

I went into Chuck's office the next morning and told him sheepishly that I quit. I wanted to do that "All the Time Fitness" thing Dave was rambling about. Chuck basically slapped me on the back and said, "Good, you can be our first franchisee." "Okay," I said. And then I drove home and wondered what the hell I just committed to. I was 26.

Opening the first Anytime Fitness location, I think a lot of members expected me to be out of business within a year. I also remember feeling the most scared, elated, anxious, depressed, steadfast, and determined I had ever been in my life—and that was my first week in business.

Eventually, I settled in. But after opening my third gym, I found myself stopping by HQ a lot more often. Between operating my own clubs and being the guru for new franchisees, I missed the daily interaction with Chuck, Dave, and others. One day when I was maybe hanging out a bit too long, Chuck said, "Don't you have some gyms to run?" I said, "Well, based on my last cell phone bill, you guys should be paying me to sell new franchises and help your franchisees get up and running." I was kidding, but Chuck said okay. Next thing you know, I'm working at Corporate doing exactly what I had just described. Fast-forward a few years, and I'm now the vice president of International Operations for a franchise whose reach spreads to 30 countries.

Between franchising my own clubs and coming back to work a corporate job, experiences have been my ultimate profits. I made good money as a franchisee, but it's always been more about the journey. I've met some of the most interesting and influential people on the planet. I've been to places rarely seen by Americans, and my experiences have made a profound impact on who I am and how I think about the world.

I've literally gone from pushing a mop and bucket to traveling the world and helping thousands of gym owners and members get to a healthier place. That's more rewarding than I ever could have imagined.

— PART IV —

Play

"The master in the art of living
Draws no sharp distinction between
His work and his play;
His labor and his leisure;
His mind and his body;
His education and his recreation.
He hardly knows which is which.
He simply pursues his vision of excellence
Through whatever he is doing,
And leaves others to determine
Whether he is working or playing.
To himself, he always appears to be doing both."

—L.P. Jacks

Formative Play Moment

•

It's a gorgeous July afternoon in 2009, and we're in a field behind our headquarters, sitting on horseback wearing long wigs, face paint, and purple kilts. We're not sure which of us came up with this idea two months ago, but as we look around, it's hard not to second-guess it.

We're shooting a video for our upcoming franchisee conference, and the idea is to re-create the famous battle scene from *Braveheart.* Except that instead of William Wallace and the Scots taking on the evil English, it's the brave warriors of Anytime Fitness—in white T-shirts emblazoned with "Passion," "Determination," "Energy," etc.—battling the insidious black-shirted forces of "Pizza," "Diabetes," "Apathy," and "The TV Remote."

We still like the idea, but we're also coming to grips with the fact that we've pulled dozens of our people away from their desks to do a day-long parody video in the middle of the week. As we wait for the director to yell "action," we can't help but think about the total expense of this venture and wonder how in the world we're going to make that money back.

But as the day goes on, a funny thing happens. Even though we're making this video to entertain and inspire our club owners, we're seeing an authentic passion take over our team. People from different departments are laughing together, getting to know each other, bonding over the experience, and buying wholeheartedly into the "good vs. evil" idea. When everybody shouts "Freedom! Anytime! Fitness!" at the end of the video, we can tell they really mean it.

After the shoot, we see these new connections breed more collaboration at work. It's obvious in the hallways and in meetings: something in our culture has improved virtually overnight. And when we show "Saveheart" at our conference, the tribal impact it has on our audience blows us away. Our franchisees laugh at the funny parts (especially Chuck's horrendous Scottish accent), but they also get caught up in the message—cheering and chanting with the characters. The entire video becomes a rallying cry for our business and our mission.

At the end of the conference in Atlanta, our franchisees are energized like never before (Chuck was so inspired, he even got his first tattoo). Eight years later, our employees still talk about "Saveheart." Franchisees will occasionally break into chants of "Freedom! Anytime! Fitness!" at our conferences. And we still don the purple kilts—not only at conferences but also for photo shoots and other speaking opportunities. We might get a few sideways glances, but to us, it symbolizes tribal passion, the fight to get to a

LOVE WORK

The 'Saveheart' Shoot

healthier place, and the joy of being part of something bigger than ourselves. Most of all, it reminds us to have a sense of play.

Since that seminal filming event, we've made conference videos every year. We've personally played the likes of Kirk and Spock, Prince and Bruce Springsteen, and Sonny and Cher, but more importantly, these productions have featured dozens of our employees and club owners from around the world. The videos are silly, but they're critical in setting the 4P tone for our annual conference. In a very real way, they help our employees and gym owners buy into our bigger mission. Mostly, they remind us of the cardinal rule of play and of life: Take what you do seriously, but never take yourself too seriously.

—Chuck & Dave

LOVE WORK

From the "Star Trek" video: Chuck as Spock and Dave as Captain Kirk

From the "Lip Sync Battle" video: Chuck as Prince, Dave as The Boss, Dave and Chuck as Sonny and Cher

In this P (Play) section:

- We'll explore the many types and benefits of play.

- We'll offer a cautionary tale from our own experiences—and talk about how to "play it right."

- We'll share a valuable outside perspective from a prominent leader who believes that the key to solving the world's biggest problems is to make finding solutions more fun.

---

[12] "Why Employee Satisfaction Matters to Shareholders," Knowledge@Wharton, September 29, 2014, http://knowledge.wharton.upenn.edu/article/why-employee-satisfaction-matters-shareholders/.

— CHAPTER 13 —

The Benefits of Play

> "We don't stop playing because we grow old. We grow old because we stop playing."
>
> —George Bernard Shaw

Long before we started Anytime Fitness, we made work fun. Why? The better question is *why the hell not?*

The average year features 262 days on the job. Even if you deduct 20 days for vacation or personal time, you're still left with 242 working days. The average American spends 8.8 hours a day on "work and related activities," so that means the average person works 2,100 hours a year.[13] Add it all up, and we spend more time with our co-workers than we do with family and friends. And yet, as we've previously mentioned, over two-thirds of us are disengaged at work. If you're one of those people, we feel sorry for you, because we can't imagine dedicating most of your life to something you don't enjoy, or even actively dislike.

But what if work could be different? What if those 242

days were a gratifying and enriching experience? What if your job brought out the very best in you? And what if work could actually be fun?

This is what we've always strived for at Anytime Fitness. In our earliest years—when we had only a handful of people in our West St. Paul office—play revolved around caffeine and competition. Every morning, the three partners would settle into coffee talks. And every afternoon, we'd engage in heated games of Ping-Pong. Most of our conversations had nothing to do with the business, yet plenty of good business ideas and decisions came out of them.

The point is: Play comes naturally to children, so why shouldn't it come naturally to adults? As a baby, you're not thinking about the evolutionary reason why you like to play peekaboo. And as an adult, you don't always realize how a party or a game improves your work performance. But it does. And that's why your business can't fire on all cylinders if your culture doesn't include a healthy dose of play.

Forms of Play

Not all play is the same, and over the years, we've seen at least four different kinds that are particularly useful in the workplace:

1. **Productive Play.**
   The best examples of this kind of play are creative forms of brainstorming or problem-solving. Productive play is critical to innovation, because it boosts engagement. As one of our team members recently said about her early days with the

company, "I'll never forget Chuck giving our executive team a speech about giving feedback. Phrases like 'we pay you to know what's in your brain,' 'if you have ideas, we want to hear them,' and 'let's just get in a room and whiteboard the possibilities' were music to my ears." When you start by asking "what's possible?" then you open people's minds to offer silly ideas that just might lead to brilliant solutions.

2. **Team-Building Play.**
While all forms of play tend to bring people together, some kinds are especially useful in building or strengthening teams within your organization. Team-building play can include on- or off-site parties, volunteer and charity events out in your community, or team-based events you might have inside your organization.

3. **Sense-of-Humor Play.**
Having a good sense of humor is an important trait in any person, but it's especially important in business (as we noted in the People section, we even look for it during the interview process). Part of being an effective leader is being approachable and able to disarm others. People are drawn to leaders who are quick to laugh, as it shows an elevated emotional intelligence—especially when you can laugh at yourself. When everyone feels secure in themselves and others, then you achieve a comfort level almost like a comedy roast, where playful ribbing is taken as a compliment. This kind of play is especially good for defusing tension in group meetings, and it truly does start at the top. If you can be thick-skinned and self-deprecating as a leader, then you can create a healthy climate where people will feel freer to contribute ideas.

4. **Competitive Play.**

We talked in the People section about how we seek out people with a competitive streak, and that's because we think of ourselves as corporate athletes. Anytime Fitness is our team, and we have opponents who want to destroy us almost as much as we want to destroy them. In the early days of Anytime Fitness, Ping-Pong was our main competitive outlet, and it was mostly healthy—even if the paddles often ended up embedded in the wall. Today our employees have many more competitive outlets, and we've enjoyed company sporting events around KnockerBall, golf, basketball, kickball, softball, and other sports.

How you approach play in your organization is obviously up to you, but at Anytime Fitness, we see it most clearly in our conference videos, Halloween and holiday parties, company sporting events, potlucks and barbecues, Tough Mudders and Warrior Dashes, and occasional field trips designed to help people overcome their fears—like that day we took some employees skydiving.

In addition to these larger, company-sponsored events, we maintain the smaller touches as well. In keeping with our roots, we still have a Ping-Pong table. And in the "rogue" category, we've always had a vibrant practical-joke culture—such as the day when Chuck found that every time he typed his name, it came up "Chunk," and every time he typed in "Shannon" (his wife's name), it came up "Sugar Mama." (Our employees apparently lack a healthy fear of being fired . . .)

But perhaps our favorite play event is a tradition we started years ago at the company holiday party. We call it "employee skits" or "rookie talent shows." Basically, every employee who joined us that year has to perform a short skit for their peers. The subject matter of these skits is wide open. And although we encourage people to be tasteful, we also encourage healthy doses of good-natured political incorrectness, especially when it comes to poking fun at leadership.

The parameters are simple. New employees are told to be prepared for the following:

- At the holiday party, you will be invited on stage.

- Introduce yourself and state your role in the company and the department you work in.

- In one minute or less, convey something unique about yourself. We encourage stupid human tricks, singing, dancing, jokes, musical instruments, impersonations, or whatever talent you want to share. Yes, you can bring props.

- Please refrain from using offensive language, behavior, or gestures. Have fun, but be professional.

Over the years, we've seen an amazing variety of performances in these skits. People have sung, played instruments, told jokes, juggled, performed magic tricks, spoken different languages, and even started a flash mob dance. More often than not, they've revealed something about themselves that others didn't know.

We know we're not grooming anyone for *Saturday Night Live* here, so we don't care about actual talent. In a way, the point of these skits is the opposite of a hazing ritual. They work because they push people out of their comfort zones in a friendly, safe, supportive, and embarrassment-free environment in which bravery is rewarded. In the end, they provide a layered experience that benefits our culture and business in multiple ways. At the end of the day, they:

- Break the ice, breed friendships, and create community.
- Celebrate everyone's uniqueness.
- Give people permission to be themselves, and be ridiculous.
- Encourage laughter with other people, showing the benefits of not taking yourself too seriously.
- Encourage and reward vulnerability, which leads to personal growth.
- Build up people's courage, which in turn gives them more confidence to speak up, question, and share ideas in meetings.
- Are fun to do, and even more fun to watch.

Whatever you do at your organization, a healthy dose of play has the power to boost your culture and business performance in multiple ways. In our case, play has improved five elements vital to a vibrant culture: creativity, collaboration, connection, employee engagement, and employee retention. *Remember: Play is freedom. And when you feel free, you (literally) perform.*

Healthy Conflict

Good leadership sometimes comes down to the complex art of managing contradiction. And while the 4 Ps are generally complementary and overlapping (especially people and purpose), we recognize that leaders can sometimes experience a certain tension between profits and play. In our experience, this is totally natural. In fact, it's healthy.

Most business leaders, including us, operate from both sides of their metaphorical brains. And these hemispheres often engage in a serious tug-of-war. The right brain tends to say "yes!" while favoring creativity and fun, whereas the left brain often screams "no!" as it pushes common sense and logical analysis.

Before shooting the "Saveheart" video, for example, the left-brain/right-brain argument in both of our heads went something like this:

Right Brain

Wouldn't it be hilarious to spoof Braveheart in a video for franchisees? We should totally do that.

Based on that, we greenlit the idea. Then on the day of the shoot, the Left Brain started to protest:

Left Brain

Are you nuts? Look at all the full-time employees in this field. Brian from accounting is dressed up as a slice of pepperoni pizza. Janet from marketing is a giant beer can. Multiply all these people by an average day's pay, add the production costs on top of that, and you're spending tens of thousands of dollars on this thing!

To which the Right Brain responded:

Right Brain
Yeah, but aren't you having fun? I mean, who else gets to spend an entire workday sitting on a horse and spouting a bunch of inside jokes in a bad Scottish accent? Look at your employees. They're having a blast. You think they're NOT going to go home and tell everyone that they have the best job ever?

Eventually, both sides come to an agreement:

Left Brain & Right Brain
You can't quantify passion, but if you could, the gains in productivity and reduction in turnover alone have definitely blown away the costs of that video. This investment delivered huge ROI. And most important, it was fun.

Most business leaders can identify with this internal argument. Like the two sides of your brain, profits and play often battle each other. Sometimes they come to an agreement; other times they don't. And that's fine. Our only advice is this: Do your best to stop thinking of profits and play as mutually exclusive. The dividends of play don't always show up on the balance sheet. And an overly serious, "unplayful" culture can exert costs in morale, retention, and productivity that can also be hard to see—and dangerous.

That being said, recent studies are starting to quantify the impact of play in a business environment—and the benefits are getting harder and harder to ignore.

The Science of Play

"There is good evidence that if you allow employees to engage in something they want to do, which is playful, there are better outcomes in terms of productivity and motivation."

—Dr. Stuart Brown, founder of the National Institute for Play

The precise financial impact of play within your organization can be difficult to determine, but a growing body of research is connecting the dots between play, happiness, and productivity. For example, studies show that:

- Happy employees are **12% more productive** than unhappy employees.[14]

- Unhappy employees cost US businesses **$300 billion** each year.[15]

- Happy salespeople produce **37% greater sales** than unhappy employees.[16]

- The happiest employees take **66% less sick leave** than those who are least happy.[17]

- Companies with happy employees outperform the competition by **20%** and are more likely to solve difficult problems faster.[18]

Research points to the fact that there are six fundamental reasons why people work, and interestingly, one of them is play.[19] Some human motivation stems from the negative (we work only for money, or out of fear), but others are rooted in the positive. Of those, a sense of play is the most enjoyable. Why? Because by definition, play is about doing something for the pure enjoyment of it.

But play isn't mindless. In fact, it's the exact opposite. Play can be a process of "sculpting the brain" by simulating situations and experiences we might find in real life. In a way, play is a form of practice—or, to use a fitness analogy, training. Play is also directly linked with curiosity, experimentation, and exploring challenging problems. Most of the challenges we come up against at work require creative thought to overcome them. Engaging in play gets our creative juices flowing, while also breaking us out of bad habits or ineffective approaches that keep us from achieving our full potential.

The Emotion of Play

One thing the science doesn't capture—but that we've witnessed for decades in the fitness industry—is how important play is to family relationships. As we look at our member success stories over the years, we start to notice patterns in the recurring moments that finally push people to get in shape. We think of these as "fitness tipping points," and without a doubt, the most common one is a medical crisis: A doctor tells someone that if they don't lose weight soon, they're highly likely to experience a heart attack or stroke. Or after failing to see results with prescription drugs or other therapies, someone gives exercise a try and discovers that it can help lift them out of depression, overcome their eating disorder, and blunt their addictions.

But another common fitness tipping point might surprise you. Time after time, we've talked to Anytime Fitness members who say that they committed to getting a gym membership the moment they realized that they were too out of shape to play with their kids. Anytime Fitness member Teri Kratz of Springfield, Minnesota, provides a perfect example. The subject of one of our first video Member Success Stories, Teri was finally moved to improve her fitness when her daughter asked her to come out to the swing set in their back yard, and Teri realized that she no longer fit in the swing. The memory of it still brings tears to her eyes.

Stories like these abound: people not being able to get on an amusement park ride, realizing that they can't take part in a game of hide-and-go-seek, or feeling winded after a simple game of catch in the backyard. Play is such a fundamental family activity—and such an important human need—that the inability to do it can break our hearts. Luckily, play also provides a primal motivator for improving our bodies and minds.

If you do it right.

---

[13] American Time Use Survey, Bureau of Labor Statistics. Accessed May 29, 2017. https://www.bls.gov/tus/charts/.

[14] Eric Siu, "It Really Pays to Have a Rich Company Culture," Entrepreneur, October 21, 2014, www.entrepreneur.com/article/238640.

[15] "What Your Disaffected Workers Cost," Gallup, March 15, 2001, www.gallup.com/businessjournal/439/what-your-disaffected-workers-cost.aspx.

[16] "Why Happiness at Work Is Important," Growth Engineering. Accessed May 29, 2017. www.growthengineering.co.uk/why-happiness-at-work-is-important/.

[17] Vicki Salemi, "Start Smiling: It Pays to Be Happy at Work," Forbes, August 14, 2010, www.forbes.com/2010/08/13/happiest-occupations-workplace-productivity-how-to-get-a-promotion-morale-forbes-woman-careers-happiness.html.

[18] Eric Siu, "It Really Pays to Have a Rich Company Culture," Entrepreneur, October 21, 2014, www.entrepreneur.com/article/238640.

[19] Neel Doshi and Lindsay McGregor, Primed to Perform: How to Build the Highest-Performing Cultures Through the Science of Total Motivation, 2015. (The other five are potential, purpose, emotional, economic, and inertia.)

— CHAPTER 14 —

Playing It Right

> *"Dave, we've made a terrible mistake."*
> —Chuck

For all the benefits of play, it can also backfire. Like anything in the workplace, there's a right way and wrong way to do it, and you shouldn't come away from this book thinking that creating a playful culture is as simple as making a parody video.

Most importantly, having a healthy sense of play in the office shouldn't be confused with forced play. If you've spent any time working in a cubicle-filled corporation (or watched the movie *Office Space*), then you know what we're talking about. Building morale by forcing compliance with Hawaiian Shirt Day, demanding attendance at cake-cutting birthday parties for employees who barely know (or actively dislike) each other, or thinking that doughnuts and a box of gourmet coffee will solve serious departmental communications issues . . . well, these aren't tactics that will foster a genuine and productive sense of play in the office.

For play to work, it has to be authentic to your company. And for anything to be authentic, people need to feel like they have a stake in it. Your goal isn't to legislate play; it's to create an environment that honors it and encourages people to express themselves through it.

Taking Play Too Far

So far, our stories of play at Anytime Fitness have sounded pretty rosy. And the vast majority of them are. But in the spirit of full disclosure, we have experienced occasional moments when maybe, just maybe, our sense of play clouded our judgment. Since you learn as much from your failures as you do from your successes, we'll share one of those stories.

In 2011, we had started to feel a general sense of jadedness when it came to fitness marketing. We were tired of the traditional approach, in which you pump out commercials, newspaper ads, and direct-mail postcards filled with happy, smiling people on treadmills—usually models who are already in great shape to begin with and bear little resemblance to the people you're actually trying to win over.

As entrepreneurs who thrived on breaking the rules and going against the grain, we wanted to reject this approach and do something fresh and controversial. So we got caught up in the idea of talking about fitness using a form of brutal honesty. "No one smiles on a treadmill unless they're watching *Caddyshack* on their iPad" went our thinking. "The truth is, working out is hard.

Working out is grueling. Working out *sucks*!"

In a way, we still agree with this approach. For all but a small minority of people, exercise isn't "fun." You may like the results, but few people love the process. And there's nothing wrong with that. Name one thing in life worth achieving that's easy. You can't. So why not just tell the truth about it?

As a result of our thinking, we crafted several marketing messages around "relative negatives" in health and exercise. In other words: Working out sucks, but not as much as getting heart disease, living with diabetes, making less money, having less sex—all consequences of being out of shape, according to various research findings we'd seen through the years. We thought this would strike a chord with people. They would respect us for being down to earth and snapping them out of their denial, and they'd be inspired to join one of our gyms.

The first product of our radical new thinking was a book called *Working Out Sucks (And Why It Doesn't Have To)*, which included inspirational stories to get people motivated toward better health, a psychological take on overcoming the mental barriers to better fitness, and a 21-day start-up plan to get readers on the road to better health. We still believe in the merits of this book, and if you're curious about it, we encourage you to check it out on Amazon.[19]

The second product was a bit more controversial. We hired a new marketing agency, and we told them to take our "honest" approach and run with it creatively. They presented us with several ideas, including some new TV spots. A large cross-section of the company weighed in, and collectively, we chose the campaign that made us laugh the most and seemed to have the best chance of cutting through the fitness marketing clutter.

Fast-forward a few months, and Chuck is standing on a beach in Malibu, California, having another "Saveheart" moment of second thoughts—except this time, the film crew is much larger, the costs involved are exponentially higher, and the right side of his brain is in total agreement with the left. Chuck watches as actors in bathing suits try to roll an overweight man in a wet suit into the ocean—against the man's obvious protests. And Chuck knows that in a few moments, he'll be filmed looking straight into the camera lens and saying:

CHUCK
Let's face it, working out sucks. But you know what sucks more? Being mistaken for a large aquatic mammal.

•

Chuck takes out his phone, and in stark contrast to the call he made 10 years earlier from the Tennessee fitness club that we mentioned in Chapter 9 (when he discovered the final key differentiator for the Anytime Fitness model), his message this time is a little different: "Dave, we've made a terrible mistake."

That's right. In our eagerness to be edgy, provocative, and "brutally honest," we paid a production company to film a commercial in which an overweight human being is mistaken for a beached whale. It made us laugh when the writer read the script in a conference room. But when you saw the script being acted out with real human beings, it wasn't funny anymore.

Suffice it to say, we ended up killing that and a few other spots in the "Working Out Sucks" campaign. When we came to our senses, we asked ourselves some basic questions: If I'm looking for a health club, is this campaign going to make me want to join Anytime Fitness ? Am I really going to feel like this is a brand that cares about me? Most importantly: Do we really think it's okay to poke fun at people who are out of shape?

The answer to all of those questions was an emphatic "no." In a moment of weakness or insanity, we had deemed something "playful" when it wasn't. We took the idea of not taking yourself too seriously and assumed that this campaign could have the same effect on potential members. It was done in the same spirit of play as our rookie skits, where the laughter comes from a sense of unconditional love, acceptance, and community. But this wasn't our holiday party, and when we saw it in a different context, we realized that it didn't represent who we were at all.

Every leader makes mistakes. The key is admitting and correcting them as soon as possible. You could make the argument that in the end, the "beached whale" experience still paid dividends. After all, it did give us a much better understanding of our true brand vision, and it also guaranteed that we would never make the same mistake twice. Then again, we probably could have learned that lesson a little less expensively.

The Flip Side: What Works

Enough about mistakes; let's get back to accentuating the positive. In the world of Anytime Fitness, perhaps the best example of play mixed with purpose is a two-day event ("Bash Before the Stash"/"Mud-Stash") organized by franchisees John Spence, Chris Slater, and Mike Gelfgot. These guys own 20+

clubs in Indiana and Ohio, and they draw over 1,000 Anytime Fitness members to the ski slopes outside of Cincinnati every year for an experience that combines fitness, friendship, charitable causes, and a little dirty fun.

Chuck enjoys some good clean fun in the mud.

    Bash Before the Stash is a dinner fundraiser whose live and silent auctions have so far raised over $100,000 for Safe Passage, an organization dedicated to helping victims of domestic abuse. Mud-Stash—the organizers' own spin on the popular mud run format—happens the following day, providing an unforgettable bonding exercise that we've personally experienced the last two years.

These events are the largest Anytime Fitness member gatherings in the world, and it should come as no surprise to you to learn that over 20 of John, Chris, and Mike's members and staff now have Runningman tattoos. In fact, one of their trainers has the distinction of sporting the biggest Anytime Fitness tattoo in the world.

To share more about our culture of play, we asked our franchisees and employees to describe how play has filtered into their lives and businesses—and which playful elements they find most gratifying. Here's a snapshot of their answers.

Dale Long's "largest tattoo"

"I love the conference spoof videos. How many companies invest in making a movie with their employees every year? The staff look forward to videos like 'Saveheart' and 'I'm Healthy & I Know It,'[20] and they're so proud when they're shown at the conference. These are also a 'show and share' moment for our friends and families. I've had so many spouses and parents come up to me and thank us for the environment we create for their loved ones. Most people can't get their head around how much fun we have."

"Most companies put on a conference in their home city or Las Vegas. We pick super-unique locations that our owners would probably never choose on their own, and that allows them to add a few vacation days on the front or back end. Our franchisees are climbing mountains in Montana, doing ropes courses, riding in helicopters, jumping out of planes, dancing at Navy Pier in '80s costumes, and tubing down ski jumps in Lake Placid. This is a part of what keeps us and them so energized throughout the year. We always have something to look forward to. We've created something so big that people want to be part of it."

"Play is important, and the clubs we own use it with team meetings and social events we do annually, as well as in our communication and environment with the team members at our clubs. We personally live with a great balance of work and play. Our encouragement to those we come in contact with is to pursue their dream to create a great balance of play. While this gets defined differently, as it should, our play is heavily weighted with travel. We take 11 trips a year, and while we work for some part of each vacation, our personal passion is for travel, so this is a priority."

"After seven years of working nonstop in the gyms I own, someone suggested that I work a little less and start playing a little more. This was easier said than done, as I love what I do. It's my baby, and I always think my business won't operate without me. In reality, with the team I have in place, it has and does. Since that advice, I've been to Europe, taken many trips in the US, and just booked a trip to Australia and New Zealand. I'm enjoying my life to the fullest. I enjoy helping others in need and support members and staff in any way I can."

"Every day, I go to work with my best friend and business partner in Anytime Fitness franchising: my wife. I view play as the ability to have time to play outside of work and time with my kids and the rest of my family. Last summer, our whole family decided to live on a houseboat, and it has become one of our favorite family memories. Thanks to the lifestyle and sense of play at Anytime, our kids will never suffer from lack of adventure; in fact, it's what they're used to!"

> "We're great at play. At our Anytime Fitness, you can always find people joking, laughing, and socializing. We're not the gym where everyone puts on their headphones and keeps to themselves. We're interactive with our members on social media, and we love to keep things fun. We recently had a Battle of the Trainers contest, where 18 of our club members participated on teams and lost a combined 468 pounds in 12 weeks. Each week there was a winning team, which kept the contest fun. We've had over a dozen of our members get the Runningman tattoo, and we always go in groups and spend the day together."

> "In terms of play, many of us still feel like we're the underdog. We still feel young and new, with so much opportunity to impact our franchisees and members. We're still a scrappy little team, putting our best players on the field and cheering like hell when they make a good play. We never miss a practice and study a lot of game film. We look at the scoreboard less. We'll probably never delay the game due to excessive celebration after a good play. But we'll never miss an opportunity to cheer or high-five our team members."

---

[19] https://www.amazon.com/Working-Out-Sucks-Doesnt-Have/dp/0738215694

[20] This one is on YouTube if you want to look it up.

— CHAPTER 15 —

An Outside Perspective: Dr. Peter Diamandis

"Designing fun, challenging games with strong incentives is a great way to foster collaboration, imagination, and innovation."

Dr. Peter Diamandis, New York Times best-selling author, founder of XPRIZE Foundation, and co-founder of Human Longevity, Planetary Resources

If there's a face of productive play, it's Dr. Peter Diamandis. A true Renaissance Man, his résumé is probably the only one on the planet that includes the words "engineer," "physician," "entrepreneur," "pioneer," "molecular genetics," and "space travel." His secret weapon is solving big problems by encouraging an unbridled sense of imagination and creativity. And his playful mindset eventually led him to found the XPRIZE Foundation, a nonprofit organization that designs and manages public competitions to achieve "radical breakthroughs for the benefit of humanity." We talked to him about the 4 Ps, and especially the importance of play.

In general, does the idea of living at the intersection of the 4 Ps resonate with you?

Yes. People, purpose, profits, and play have been core to all of my ventures. The people in your life are critical to achieve anything. Purpose makes your ventures meaningful. Profit is a means of keeping score, and when you profit handsomely, you gain the ability to play the game again at a higher level. You channel that energy into bigger and more meaningful purposes. And play inspires creativity and imagination. They all allow you to persevere—another important P—during the difficult times. And purpose, profits, and play help you attract the best people in the world to join your team.

Growing up, did you have an "aha" moment—a personal experience around playful, creative collaboration that solved (or failed to solve) a problem?

My first company was called SEDS (Students for the Exploration and Development of Space). It was a college-based space organization that was certainly purpose-driven, and the people I worked with became my closest friends. Because of this, starting SEDS was play for me. While it was a nonprofit organization, we profited in many other ways, including gaining incredible access to amazing people and places.

This became the model for me from then on: Find something I'm extremely excited about, something that drives me. Find a team of amazing people to co-found a venture around it. Add value and build a real, profitable business. And have fun while doing it.

XPRIZE talks about "pushing the boundaries of human potential by focusing on problems currently believed to be unsolvable, or that have no clear path toward a solution." How does a sense of play foster collaboration, imagination, and innovation from a team?

I'm endlessly curious and excited about the future. The idea of shaping it is fun to me. And it's hard work. Having fun with your team is critical as a way to balance the work. Also, I love to "gamify" as much as possible. Designing fun, challenging games with strong incentives is a great way to foster collaboration, imagination, and innovation from a team. Further, in the decades ahead, experimentation is going to be critical to building an agile company. And for me, experimentation and gamification go hand in hand.

Moving to Action: Play
with Carol Grannis, Ed.D.

All you need is a journal, some uninterrupted time (30 minutes will do), and some vulnerability. Here are some exercises to get you moving forward in the area of play.

•

Carol Grannis, Ed.D., Chief Self Esteem Officer for SEB

5 Things You Can Do Right Now

1. Identify someone (or a couple of people to work together) within your business who could be the *Cultivator(s) of Play*. Have them review this section on play (heck, the whole book), and work with them on specific ways to increase play in your business.

2. Schedule a specific date (get out your calendar right now) to facilitate the "Employee Skits" event. Have everyone participate this round, and then use this activity with new employees moving forward.

3. Write down the team-building events that your team currently participates in. Did you have some? Could you have more? Think about off-site parties, celebrations, holidays, and charity events.

4. Ask two or three of your employees how they view the amount of play in your business, and ask for their ideas on this subject.

5. As Dr. Diamandis shared, the use of challenging games can foster collaboration and innovation. Write down three ways that you can use games within your business.

Big Ideas in This Section

All work and no play? We all spend so much of our life at work. What if our work experience could be enjoyable, productive, *and* fun? This section is about the benefits of creating more joy within the workday, which equals more engaged employees. And when your employees are engaged, everything is better (productivity, creativity, service, collaboration).

Lighten up, Francis.[21] I was talking to a wonderful and successful business owner about this idea of play in the workplace, and he said, "I am not fun. I have no sense of humor. I'm nothing like Chuck and Dave. What do I do with this one?" And here's the thing: Play may resonate really strongly with you, but you may show up in the world as rather serious. Maybe you're not the originator of the jokes or the organizer of the fun, but someone in your workplace needs to help cultivate play.

The Cowardly Lion. We want courageous workplaces. When employees have courage, it leads to confidence, collaboration, creativity, and a hunger to win. We believe that a healthy sense of play supports a courageous environment, because when people can express a sense of vulnerability in a supportive environment, it leads to further growth and development.

Journaling Section

"Assess Your Joy"

- Think about the last time you experienced play at work—a time where you laughed and made powerful connections with others.

- Rate yourself on a scale of 1–10 in terms of how often you experience joy at work (1: No joy, no rainbows; 10: We could write a book about how successful we are at using play as a powerful advantage to the success of our business).

Now answer these questions:

- When was the last time I experienced joy, and what was the genesis of this happening?

- What was the outcome of this experience on me and others?

- What would make my number higher?

- What am I doing that's working?

- Who do I work with who has "easy joy"—the person who finds joy and humor in most situations?

- How could I get this person involved in helping our culture of play?

"A Little Compassion"

- If you're experiencing real-life heartaches right now and finding joy very difficult, write about it.

- If you suffer from depression like many of my own beloved family members, give yourself a dose of compassion.

- Remember that our lives are made up of seasons. Maybe this is the season of heartache for you, and you can lean on someone else to help you with play for the team.

- Consider partnering with an experienced therapist and medical doctor to offer support and optimism, because you deserve it.

Online Resources @ www.PeoplePurposeProfitsPlay.com

- Building Trust: River of Life, personal histories, and 36 questions

A Story to Tell: Tressa Dokken

It was September 16, 2011, and nothing could have prepared me for what I was about to do. Who's crazy enough to jump out of a plane at 13,000 feet when one of her greatest fears is heights? Me, apparently. Never in a hundred years did I think I would skydive. But given the opportunity (through work, of all places), it's about to happen. Maybe.

Here's how it unfolded: First, a group of us watch an educational video that looks like it was created in 1980. We go through class instruction, sign waivers, suit up, and get paired with a tandem instructor. That's the easy part. Walking across a grassy field to a small plane with three tiny propellers . . . not so much.

I crouch down to get into the plane, take a seat on a metal bench, and look through a tiny window as we fly to altitude. Coming out of a difficult time in my life, I knew I needed to shake things up, but couldn't I just go to the spa? "Why are you doing this?" I keep asking myself. I'm completely content to keep two feet on the ground, so why change it up now?

As we reach our jumping altitude, my emotions start to get the best of me. Tears run down my face. I look through that tiny window and think about which excuse I'm going to give NOT to jump. My heart races. The metal bench makes me shiver. The plane is noisy and filled with the stench of oil and exhaust. But a second later, I begin to see a different perspective through the same window: the most beautiful blue sky I've ever seen, the white clouds I'm about to jump through, the most powerful sunshine I've ever felt. My body transforms from fear to excitement. As I wipe away the tears, I turn to look at my co-workers with a big, cheesy grin on my face.

My tandem-diver tightens my straps. The doors fly open. We scoot to the edge of the plane. My feet hang over the edge. To my left, I see the outside of the plane. To my right, the big, noisy engine. Below, nothing but clouds.

And we jump.

As we free fall, my first thought is, "So this is what it's like to be a bird!" When we drop below the clouds, the parachute opens, my companion points out the amazing view of the Minneapolis skyline, and something I had feared suddenly transforms into the most peaceful and freeing feeling I've ever had.

If it weren't for this opportunity, I don't know where I would be. Sometimes you need someone or something to literally push you out of your comfort zone. Because only when you're vulnerable can you truly gain new strength and courage.

As the ground approaches and the people below no longer look like ants, I think to myself, "Once my feet hit solid ground, I will start a new chapter in my life." And I do.

A Story to Tell: Marc Conklin

Marc Conklin posing as an Anytime Fitness manager as a stuffed cat hits his office window

Every year, I take Chuck, Dave, and a handful of Anytime Fitness leaders to lunch to say "thank you" for being my first client back in 2008. But these lunches have become famous for something else: generating random and bizarre creative ideas. This was probably best demonstrated in the winter of 2010.

I had just attended a showcase called "The Best of British Advertising," and my mind was still a bit warped by the English sense of humor. I've always appreciated the fact that Brits are game to cross lines of decency that Americans consider too edgy or offensive, and I have a huge weakness for Monty Python-style absurdity. So when Chuck asked the table for ideas on how to commemorate the opening of Anytime's 1,000th gym, I quipped: "I know—let's show a cat flying into the window of an Anytime Fitness club. Then another, and another, and another. And at the end, the announcer says, 'Anytime Fitness. You can't swing a dead cat without hitting one of our clubs.'"

The idea got some laughs, and I assumed that we would quickly go back to munching on deep-fried cheese curds. But Chuck had that sideways grin coupled with a far-off look in his eye that always spells trouble. The gears were churning. "How much would that cost?" he asked. I threw out a number based on zero research, and the next thing I know, I'm sitting in an office as some poor wretch hurls stuffed cats at my window on a minus-20-degree day in January.

The result was a web-only spot that didn't win any awards but has definitely provided some internal entertainment over the years. Did the video generate greater brand awareness or inspire a single new membership? Probably not. Rather amazingly, it did generate hate mail from an animal rights organization—despite the fact that it ends with the disclaimer that "no stuffed cats were harmed in the making of this video."

Since that day, I've been fortunate to produce several ridiculous videos for Chuck, Dave, and their amazing employees and franchisees. Ridiculous spoof of the Hangover movie: check. "Star Trek: Into Fitness": check. Videos in which a treadmill uses a Barry White voice to romance people into working out: check.

No one works harder than Chuck and Dave. And it's an honor just to play in the same sandbox with two guys who are so serious about not being serious.

---

[21] For those of you too young to get the reference, this is a line from the classic 1981 Bill Murray movie *Stripes*.

— CHAPTER 16 —

Applying the 4 Ps

Today more than ever, a high-performing business runs on a high-performing culture. Like the mantra "grow or die," your culture is either getting better or it's getting worse; there's no in-between. And since we're in the fitness business, an analogy feels appropriate here.

Culture Muscles

A business culture is like the muscles in your body. Everyone has a current state of physical fitness, and physical activity is the primary power source for everything else in your life. It forms the foundation of your mood, energy, relationships, sex life, productivity, and performance. Similarly, every organization has a culture whether you consciously design it or not. As the primary power source for your business, that culture shows up in every meeting, customer interaction, hiring decision, and sales call.

Just as people tend to think that exercise is all biceps and abs, they mistakenly think that culture is little more than Bring

Your Pet to Work Day. When it comes to exercise, you can't just work out for a few weeks and then stop. If you do, your muscles get weaker, your body fat increases, and you lose everything you gained (alarmingly quickly) until atrophy sets in. In business, you can't just insert the 4 Ps and forget about them. If you don't breathe life into your culture each and every day, your ability to compete, innovate, and win will atrophy as well.

For us, the 4 Ps have become a strategic lens through which we view every aspect of our business, and against which we measure every key decision. They guided our decision in 2012 to acquire Waxing the City, a national body-waxing franchise that also runs on and delivers the promise of people, purpose, profits, and play. We use them to choose our "master franchisees": the people who control our franchise activity rights in their respective countries around the world. And as we mentioned in the Introduction, they played a pivotal role in helping us choose our equity partner, Roark Capital, as we wanted to work with someone who shared the values we outlined in our Investor Manifesto.[22]

For you, the application might be different depending on your size or industry. But keep in mind: You must embrace all four Ps, and they must work in collaboration (or, occasionally, healthy conflict) toward your decisions. Before taking any significant action, ask yourself: Does it support the idea that people are our most important asset? Does it support the larger purpose of our organization and/or the other causes that our people value? Does it contribute to our ability to compete and profit in the marketplace? And does it contribute to an authentic sense of childlike fun and play?

If you can answer yes to those questions, congratulations: You just flexed your culture muscles.

The Big Question

A few years ago, Chuck was in his office having a discussion with an Anytime Fitness employee who had been with the company from its start-up days, and who is still with us today. She had seen it all—from the era of beer and Ping-Pong to the introduction of org charts, strategic and budget planning, and the legal and HR layers that emerge as a company has more to lose and protect.

In the course of talking about the concerns that often accompany a fast-growing company and its team, this employee asked Chuck something that has stayed with us ever since:

"Would you work for your company today?"

It's a pretty basic question, but it rewired our brains. If we weren't the CEO and president of this company—if we simply wandered through the doors one day, met the people, and absorbed the culture—would we still want to work here? For us, the answer is a resounding yes. But the question gets to the heart of what drives many business leaders and entrepreneurs away, and why it's so rare for company founders to stay involved as their companies grow and mature: They either can't or don't want to adapt.

Everyone from CEOs to departmental managers should ask themselves this question regularly: Would I want to work in the company or department I've created? You can easily recall jobs you had growing up that were filled with (or devoid of) inspiration. The good ones had a sense of fun and impact. But what happens when leaders attain the power to actually shape the cultures they work in, and why don't we always re-create the ones we loved best?

In a nutshell, it's because high-performance cultures are hard to create, let alone maintain. We had the gratification of seeing our efforts pay off over time in multiple culture-related awards. But our more important work has come afterwards in our efforts to keep flexing those culture muscles. After all, being named a "number-one global franchise" or "best place to work" is great, but where do you go from #1 except down?

To nip that challenge in the bud, we released an all-staff email that we think is worth sharing. Once you move closer to achieving your own high-performance culture, we encourage you to stay hungry and communicate a message similar to this one:

Best Team in Franchising,

If an outsider was trying to uncover the foundational elements of what makes our culture remarkable, they'd likely start by studying our mission and vision statements. But while it's important to establish what our culture is, let's also discuss what remarkable culture isn't.

Remarkable culture isn't about control.
Intelligence, creativity, and passion shouldn't be suppressed, and therefore, we grant a tremendous amount of autonomy as team members problem-solve or bring new ideas to market.

Remarkable culture isn't about keeping everyone happy.
Although our employee turnover has been minimal, people have left to pursue new opportunities, and that will happen again in the years ahead. But that's okay, because as life changes, sometimes people need to climb a new mountain. We've also had to terminate people for a variety of reasons, as the strategic pivoting of a company often requires difficult personnel changes. Job satisfaction fluctuates constantly, and no company is immune to the complex range of human emotions. Despite our awards, we still have plenty of room for improvement.

Remarkable culture isn't cheap or easy.
As we grow, our culture becomes more fragile—and the difficulties are magnified with off-site team members. We know from surveys that off-site employees are less engaged than those who work inside the building. This isn't easily explained, because culture is intangible. But we also know that it can dissipate over time and distance— like watching a concert on YouTube versus being in the front row with your friends: You can still enjoy the music and admire the artistry, but you won't feel it pumping

through your body. A remarkable culture is a rich, empowering experience, and if it was easy to produce, every company would have it. That's why per employee, we reinvest more than most companies. And we remain committed to providing opportunities and resources for personal and professional growth.

Remarkable culture isn't infallible.
Every so often, someone takes advantage of our trusting culture via flex time or loose company policies around expense reports, employee travel, or employer-provided perks. At many other companies, the response from senior leadership or HR is to implement new ironclad policies to prevent this behavior. When that happens, the fertile soil of a trusting culture is slowly poisoned. So we won't stop trusting the many over the actions of the few.

Remarkable culture isn't about toga parties.
Outsiders envision us throwing constant parties with crazy shenanigans, and although we've had an actual toga party, our great culture has never been built around a party atmosphere. In fact, we used to have parties more often, and our culture wasn't nearly as strong. Now we party less and work harder, but our culture is better.

Remarkable culture is never finished.

From the outside, people see meteoric growth without the knowledge of setbacks and problems that accompany a fast-growing franchise. Most of them will never comprehend the tenacity, nimbleness, and boundless positive energy needed. Our culture awards recognize that hard work, as well as our unique approach toward people, purpose, profits, and play.

—Chuck & Dave

Steal Our Employee Value Proposition!

Perhaps the most significant aspect of our business that's been directly informed by the 4 Ps is what we call our Employee Value Proposition. This single page of text is a major tool in attracting, onboarding, and retaining employees. So to finish our part of the book, we'd like to share this document with you and encourage you to use it as a template for your own business.

If you were to strip out our specific language but keep the 4 Ps from this document, what would it look like for your business or department? Consider this as a template for finding and keeping employees but also as a touchstone for your entire culture.

Remember: The world needs more engagement, and it starts with every business leader doing their part to create high-performing cultures using the 4 Ps as their guide. We wish you the best in defeating the scourge of undertime and bringing people, purpose, profits, and play into your business and your life.

Let's all starting loving work!

Our Employee Value Proposition

When all of these factors below are considered, we believe that we offer one of the most compelling employment opportunities. Our Employee Value Proposition is defined through our People, Purpose, Profits, and Play philosophy.

People

- **We will continue to invest** in the personal and professional development of each employee. This is carried out with our focus on employee development, our professional workshops, Leadership Cohort series, and college tuition programs.

- **Flexibility:** Our goal is to provide a work environment that supports all parts of your life, and allows you to live your best life—whatever that means for you.

- **Opportunity and growth:** We'll always look for opportunities to promote from within to bring new challenges and advancement to the team. Our goal is for you to grow as our organization grows.

- **Wellness:** We want our employees to be their healthiest, which in turn fuels their lives inside and outside of work. Our campus provides a fitness center, personal trainer, outdoor trails, abundance of sunlight, and quiet areas. We believe in a body, mind, and spirit connection, and will support the ongoing learning of these areas.

- **Oh yeah**, you also get free wax services.

Purpose

- **Trust, autonomy, and impact:** The work we do matters by enriching lives, and we are committed to a workplace culture that values ideas and input from every team member. We will strive to build trust with each other and earn the trust of our franchises. Our ongoing quest will be to answer the question "Why are we here?" for our franchises and ourselves.

- **Emotional connections:** Our campus is designed to bring people together to form stronger business and personal relationships.

Profits

- **In terms of monetary compensation** (including hourly, salary, bonuses, commissions, or longer-term incentive plans), we will strive to be competitive, fair and transparent in our pay practices.

- **In terms of total compensation (pay plus benefits),** we want our benefits to be competitive and supportive of our employees. These benefits include 401(k) plans, health insurance, paid maternity/paternity leave, travel, and entertainment stipends and computer/smartphone reimbursements.

Play

- **We will continue to invest in a playful culture** with team and company parties, recognition gifts, and occasional events that may be overlooked but that add to our special culture.

Assessing Your P-ocity

with Carol Grannis, Ed.D.

Now that you know about the 4 Ps, what's your benchmark? Complete this assessment as you would a magazine quiz: Answer the questions quickly. If you want to answer the question "True-ish" or think to yourself, "I sometimes do that," then mark it as False. We're looking for consistent habits and beliefs.

1. I genuinely care about the people who work with me.

    True   False

2. I show them I care by getting to know what's important to them in their lives.

    True   False

3. I spend time developing others, and I see mistakes as an opportunity to learn.

    True   False

4. I support collaboration and teamwork in my business.

    True   False

5. I have a good process in place to welcome new employees to the business, and they learn what they need to know to be successful.

    True   False

6. I'm very clear about the purpose of my life, and I live out that purpose daily in my actions.

   True   False

7. I've clearly articulated the important purpose of my business to my team, and they could articulate the same purpose when asked.

   True   False

8. I care about the life purposes of my employees, and I make space in my business for them to ask and answer that question for themselves.

   True   False

9. I'm astute in the financial management of my business. I have a method to keep track of how we're doing and regularly make decisions based on the data.

   True   False

10. I regularly look for ways to invest in my business with a mindset for long-term success.

    True   False

11. I have designed my business to support a fulfilling life, and I find time to engage in life events that are meaningful to me.

    True   False

12. I am consistently curious about my business and industry, and I seek out ways to anticipate the needs of my customers.

    True   False

13. Having fun is an important part of my business—and is important to the people I work with.

    True   False

14. I don't take myself too seriously and genuinely laugh when others make light-hearted jokes about me.

    True   False

15. I support and engage in regular activities with my staff that promote trust, creativity, and laughter.

    True   False

Overall P-ocity Strength

Count the total number of Trues:_____

<u>Key</u>

12 to 15:   You've got this! Your P-ocity is very strong.

9 to 11:   Your P-ocity is solid, but there are some great opportunities for getting even stronger.

6 to 8:   Isn't it so great that this learning is coming to you? No harm, no foul. You have some focused work to do.

Below 6:   If this score makes you feel uncomfortable, congratulations! This discomfort will move you to action and deepen your learning more quickly than those who scored higher than you. You should be proud of your honesty and vulnerability.

Individual P-ocity Strength

Count the number of Trues you chose for each section, and write that number in the space below.

People: Questions #1–5: _____

Purpose: Questions #6–8 _____

Profits: Questions #9–12: _____

Play: Questions #13–15: _____

This scoring can show you which of your Ps are strongest. That's critical, because part of success is recognizing and leveraging your strengths. This will allow you to develop mastery in that area, differentiate yourself from others, and build your confidence.

Some Questions to Muddle On

Which of the Ps was your strongest? What's the impact of your strength in this area? On your business? On your team? On your customers?

Which section was your weakest? What's the impact of this P on your business? On your team? On your customers? What would it cost you or your business if you choose to do nothing to improve in this area? Is there someone you work with who could help you in this area? Who is it? What would the impact be if you asked that person for their help in strengthening this area?

One More Story to Tell: Brian & Lisa Bazely

When we joined the Anytime Fitness family in 2008, we did so with a desire to find more balance. We were financially well off. We had no debt, a great house, new vehicles, and a great marriage. But when we evaluated our life in 2007, we determined that the one thing missing was time. We had two beautiful daughters, both about to enter the most challenging time of their life: the teenage years. Being there for them—truly being there for them—driving them to school events, attending their sports activities, etc., would require more than regular vacation time.

The Anytime Fitness business model provided exactly what we were looking for. We could open clubs, manage the marketing and financials remotely, and not be tied to the day-to-day operations. But what really caught our attention was the 4 Ps and the tone that Chuck, Dave, and others struck about the business. They were running a business as a franchisor, but were clearly very interested in many of the same things from a balance-of-life perspective. We've since opened eight Anytime Fitness clubs and incorporated the 4 Ps into all aspects of our lives.

While family has always been important to us, our extended family at the clubs is also important. They are our people. Taking a page out of the Anytime Fitness Corporate book, we set aside money to develop them as individuals. We spend the first Friday of every month helping them grow as a team and as individuals. This includes bringing in a nutritionist, teaching them about personal finances, or helping

Brian and Lisa Bazely, Anytime Fitness' "Franchisees of the Year," 2014

them with conflict management or other competencies.

Purpose is the heart of the business. In our personal lives, helping others who are less fortunate makes everything else real. In the clubs, we change members' lives. This goes beyond providing an environment for them to work out. We've comped memberships for people going through tough financial times. We've provided free training, and we've offered complimentary memberships to family members who are in town visiting for holidays. Outside the club, we're heavily involved in the Chamber, mentorship programs, fitness-related events, and helping children in need. We put a significant effort into charities, and we're proud of the fact that our organization has purpose in everything we do.

Profits support all we do for our staff and the team's

development. While we wouldn't compromise the other Ps for this, it's the backbone of business to ensure we can grow and develop.

Play is something we use with team meetings, with annual social events, and in our communication and environment with our team members. We personally live with a great balance of work and play. Our encouragement to those we come in contact with is to pursue their dream to create a great balance of play. While this gets defined differently, as it should, our play is heavily weighted with travel.

We take 11 trips per year, and while we work for some part of each vacation, our personal passion is for travel, so this is a priority.

Looking back over the years, we've been able to impact employees and members with the 4 P philosophy. However, we've also impacted our daughters as we guide them toward entering the workforce. We want for our girls what we now have: the balance of people, purpose, profits, and play. Rather than helping them focus on a company job, the income level, and perks, we talk a lot about their time, the balance of a great income, and the flexibility to do what they want and control their lives.

Final Words of Advice

Throughout this book, we've emphasized how extraordinary leadership usually requires you to put other stakeholders' interests first. But it also requires a dose of selfishness. So to borrow from the often-used metaphor of "putting the oxygen mask on yourself before helping others," here's a checklist of what you need to do every day to be a truly effective leader in any context.

1. Improve your body intelligence by feeding, moving, and resting your body properly. The link between emotional and physical health, financial wealth, and mental acuity is well proven. Don't think it somehow doesn't apply to you.

2. Know yourself. Dave is an extrovert and recharges by talking through situations. Chuck is an ambivert and often needs quiet time to recharge. Always be aware of what provides and replenishes your energy.

3. Build your self-awareness muscle. Ask for feedback regularly and engage in 360-degree evaluations from your peers. You *can* handle the truth.

4. Be a lifelong student by learning every day through books, podcasts, seminars, or simply listening to someone else's perspective. The minute we stop being curious is the moment we stop growing.

5. Find moments to disconnect from technology. Seriously, put down your phone (unless you're reading this book on it).

6. Take time to reflect and work *on* your life and business, not in it. Remember, your business needs to be designed to support your life, not the other way around.

7. Surround yourself with friends and family who bring you happiness and nudge you to be a better person.

8. Engage in hobbies that bring you joy.

9. Do activities that push you beyond your comfort zone.

10. Live at the center of people, purpose, profits, and play.

Chuck Runyon
CEO and Co-Founder of Anytime Fitness and Self Esteem Brands

With more than 25 years of experience managing, owning, and franchising health clubs, Chuck Runyon has distinguished himself as a leading authority in the field of fitness. Runyon revolutionized the industry when he and Dave Mortensen co-founded Anytime Fitness—an alternative to big-box gyms that typically feature expensive "frills" that few members actually use or need. In contrast, Runyon and Mortensen designed smaller neighborhood clubs featuring the things members want most: convenience, affordability, quality equipment, and surprisingly personable service in friendly, nonintimidating facilities.

For his unprecedented and unique contributions to the fitness industry, Runyon was honored as the "John McCarthy Industry Visionary of the Year" by the International Health, Racquet, and

Sportsclub Association (IHRSA) in 2009. More recently, Runyon was honored by *Chief Executive* magazine with its inaugural Leadership Award for his commitment to investing in people and relationships. Specifically noted were Runyon's efforts to help his employees become not merely more productive workers but also better people. Central to his leadership philosophy is the concept of "ROEI": the return on *emotional* investment characterized by an emphasis on people, purpose, profits, and play.

Recognized as an expert on eliminating the barriers to healthy lifestyles, Runyon is frequently asked to speak or comment on issues related to why people claim that their health is a top priority, while typically spending less than 1 percent of their time exercising.

Under Runyon's leadership, Anytime Fitness has earned numerous industry accolades, including "#1 Franchise in the World," according to *Entrepreneur* magazine; "One of America's Most Promising Companies," according to *Forbes*; and the "Fastest-Growing Fitness Club in the World," according to IHRSA. Additionally, Anytime Fitness has been honored as a "Top Franchise for Minorities" and "The Best Place to Work in Minnesota" four years in a row.

Dave Mortensen

President and Co-Founder of Anytime Fitness and Self Esteem Brands

From cleaning equipment to selling memberships to co-founding the world's fastest-growing fitness franchise, Dave Mortensen has done just about everything you can do in the fitness industry. That wide-ranging experience has helped him become one of the world's leading experts on helping others "Get to a Healthier Place." Mortensen is a rock-solid athlete, but his heartfelt practice of emotional intelligence has earned him a reputation among his co-workers and throughout the fitness industry as a thoughtful and generous leader.

In the early days of Anytime Fitness, Mortensen helped spur the company's growth by overseeing the development and implementation of its integrated security, surveillance, usage-tracking, and reciprocity systems. These days, he's heavily involved in Anytime Fitness' evolution from a gym that emphasizes simple convenience to one that offers around-the-clock coaching services, utilizing the latest technology to provide members with support, nutritional information, and a wide array of new fitness training programs. Mortensen also continues to play an important role in leading the expansion of Anytime Fitness worldwide, frequently traveling to consult with master franchisees in faraway countries like Australia, Japan, and China.

The first Anytime Fitness gym opened its doors in Cambridge, Minnesota, in May 2002. In the years since, Anytime Fitness has quickly become an international powerhouse—with more than 3,500 gyms located in all 50 states and nearly 30 countries on five continents, serving 3 million members.

Under Mortensen's leadership, Anytime Fitness has earned numerous industry accolades, including "One of America's Most Promising Companies," "Top Global Franchise," "Fastest-Growing Fitness Club," a "Top Franchise for Minorities," and for four consecutive years, "The Best Place to Work in Minnesota."

Marc Conklin
Conk Creative LLC

Marc Conklin is a screenwriter, copywriter, executive ghostwriter/editor, and musician who left the ad agency world at the start of the Great Recession as a way of proving his independence and impeccable timing. When he answered his first phone call as Conk Creative LLC in January 2008, Chuck Runyon was on the other line. Since that moment, Marc has had a front-row seat to witness the growth and accomplishments of Anytime Fitness. And he has been profoundly grateful for the chance to collaborate with Chuck, Dave, and the entire Anytime Fitness team for almost 10 years.

In addition to working on business books and dozens of TV, radio, and web spots, Marc penned the indie film *Memorial Day* starring James Cromwell, which won multiple film festival awards and played on national television for four years starting in 2012.

Marc's personal writing has appeared in magazines and literary journals, including *Notre Dame Magazine* and *Water~Stone Review*. His latest music project, "Just Can't Sing," will be available on iTunes® in late 2017.

Marc has a BA from the University of Notre Dame and an MFA in creative writing from Hamline University. He lives in St. Paul, Minnesota, with his wife, Anne, their son, James, and their golden retriever/chow chow, Goldy.

More Information

For information on becoming an Anytime Fitness or Waxing the City franchisee, to inquire about hiring Chuck and Dave for conferences and speaking engagements, or to learn more about the HeartFirst Charitable Foundation™, visit the Self Esteem Brands website at:

www.selfesteembrands.com